THE MISSING CREW

A SELF-HELP GUIDE FOR MEN TO MAKE FRIENDS, END LONELINESS, AND BUILD REAL FRIENDSHIPS IN ADULTHOOD

BEN HOLLOWAY

CONTENTS

INTRODUCTION

There's a quiet moment most men recognize, even if they've never put language to it.

It's late, the house has settled into silence, and your phone lights up. You pick it up almost automatically, scrolling without expectation. Messages pass by. Notifications blur together. Names that once carried weight sit untouched, shaped by time doing what time always does. Life filled up. Distance took form. Somewhere along the way, you realized there wasn't anyone you'd call just to talk.

This is how it happens for most men.

Friendship rarely disappears in a single moment. It thins and stretches as seasons change, as routines adjust, as responsibility accumulates.

- Moves take place.
- Careers shift.
- Relationships deepen.
- Children arrive.
- Work moves indoors.

Weeks roll into months, months settle into years, and the crew you assumed would always exist gradually slips into memory. That realization carries a quiet weight, one that many men feel but rarely articulate.

What you're experiencing speaks less about personal failure and more about the world that formed around you. Modern life has reshaped the conditions under which male friendship once grew naturally. What used to emerge from proximity and repetition now requires intention.

For generations, connections had formed through shared ground, schools, workplaces, neighborhoods, churches, and teams. Men showed up, saw the same faces, and bonds developed without effort. Over time, those structures weakened. Mobility increased, digital life expanded, work followed people home, and community shifted from something embedded to something optional.

Then the pandemic accelerated everything. Isolation moved from occasional to structural. Offices emptied, casual conversations dissolved, and habits narrowed. Suddenly, remote work offered freedom and flexibility, yet quietly removed the friction points that once created connection without planning. For many men, relationships did not return in the same way they left. What felt temporary hardened into a pattern. The body noticed before the mind caught up.

Across the world, men die younger than women, and the gap is wider than most realize. In nearly every country, men make up the overwhelming majority of suicide deaths. In many places, suicide remains one of the leading causes of death for men under forty-five, outpacing accidents, illness, and violence. The pattern repeats across continents, cultures, and economies, whether in highly developed nations or developing ones. Men are several times more likely than women to die by suicide in countries like the United States, the United Kingdom, Australia, Russia, and Argentina, and in a significant portion of the world, the rates among men reach levels that are seldom seen among women (Schumacher, 2019).

Alongside this, men experience depression, anxiety, and chronic stress at staggering rates, yet speak about it far less and seek support far later. Many never name what they're carrying until it shows up in their health, their relationships, or their breaking point. These aren't abstract figures or distant headlines. They are lived realities unfolding in quiet apartments, long commutes, late nights, and lives carried under pressure. This is the cost of enduring alone.

Men learn how to function, how to provide, how to absorb strain, yet rarely how to distribute it. Over time, the load grows heavier. Isolation deepens. Suffering becomes a private matter rather than a shared healing experience. Silence settles in, not because men lack depth, but because they were never shown a workable way through it.

That silence has lasted long enough.

I wrote this because I've watched what that silence does to men. I've seen capable, intelligent men shrink their worlds quietly, convincing themselves they were fine while carrying more than they ever named. I've felt the weight of conversations that never happened, friendships that faded without closure, and the cost of assuming strength meant handling everything alone. At some point, it became clear that insight without instruction wasn't enough, and that men didn't need more commentary; they needed a way through.

Awareness is where change begins. You notice the pattern. You recognize the toll. You understand that strength loses meaning when it shortens your life, drains your joy, and limits your capacity to show up fully for the people who depend on you. From awareness comes identification, naming what's missing. From identification comes assimilation, learning how the connection actually forms. From assimilation comes distribution, building rhythms of friendship that circulate support instead of containing strain.

This is the shift that matters.

For years, the conversation around male loneliness has circled the problem without offering men anything they could actually use. Plenty of words, plenty of awareness, very little guidance that fits real life. What's been missing is something actionable, something that works with limited time, changing seasons, and the way men actually build trust and connection.

The pages that follow are shaped for the world as it exists now, for men navigating responsibility, time pressure, shifting seasons, and lives that look stable from the outside while feeling increasingly isolated within. This is for the remote worker whose days blur together, the father whose circle has shrunk as his responsibilities have grown, the man starting over after loss or relocation, and anyone who senses that something essential has gone missing. What unfolds here is a grounded framework built around how adult male friendship truly works.

You'll see how connection forms gradually, how momentum begins and fades, and how small, consistent moves build something steady over time. The approach is practical and sequential, showing how to move from acquaintance to real friendship, when to lean in or pull back, and how to build rhythms that last rather than one-off efforts. You'll recognize opportunities hiding in plain sight, learn language that feels natural to use, and develop patterns that hold even as life continues to change. Along the way, you'll encounter stories from men who rebuilt connection quietly, through rhythm rather than reinvention.

This is something you return to as life shifts. You enter where you are, apply what fits, and revisit it when the season changes again. If something in you recognizes the quiet space where connection could live more fully, trust that recognition. It isn't a weakness, it's clarity.

You don't need a massive circle or constant momentum. You need something real, something steady, something built with intention.

You need a crew, and you can build one.

This starts with one honest look at where you are, followed by small, deliberate steps taken consistently. You don't do this perfectly, and you don't do it alone either. You walk through it alongside someone who understands the terrain and is committed to helping you build something that holds.

CHAPTER 1:
THE FRIENDSHIP GAP

"The most terrible poverty is loneliness, and the feeling of being unloved." - Mother Teresa

A man can go an entire week without speaking to another man about anything that matters. Not because there's no one around, but because nothing in his week requires it. Work meetings stay transactional. Messages stay brief. Conversations orbit tasks, deadlines, and logistics. Days pass without friction, without interruption, without the kind of contact that reminds you that you're part of something shared.

For many men, this becomes normal before it ever becomes noticeable. In fact, for most of human history, men did not have to search for community because they were born inside it. In villages, tribes, towns, and early cities, life was organized around shared survival and shared purpose. Men worked the same land, defended the same borders, built the same roads, and answered to the same rhythms of day and season. Connection wasn't a goal, it was a condition of living.

Across cultures, this pattern repeated. In many African societies, men were shaped within age sets, extended families, and communal labor, growing alongside the same peers from youth into elderhood. In parts of Europe and early America, men formed bonds through guilds, churches, militias, farms, and trades, often working shoulder to shoulder for decades. Even during war, hardship, and scarcity, men were bound together by necessity, responsibility, and shared consequence.

Belonging was reinforced by repetition. You saw the same men daily, relied on them, argued with them, celebrated with them, and buried with them. Community wasn't something you maintained; it maintained you.

Over time, progress reshaped this arrangement. Industrialization pulled men away from extended kin and into cities. Modern economies rewarded mobility over rootedness. Individual success slowly replaced collective continuity. Generation by generation, the structures that once anchored male connection loosened.

The twentieth century accelerated the shift.

- Work became specialized, then portable.
- Neighborhoods became temporary.
- Families became smaller and more dispersed.
- Technology promised efficiency and freedom, yet quietly reduced the need for shared physical presence.

Men gained independence, but lost continuity. What emerged looked like an advancement. Careers expanded, lifestyles improved, and choices multiplied, yet beneath that progress, something essential thinned. Without enduring communal structures, connection became optional rather than assumed. Friendship moved from environment into effort, from rhythm into something you had to remember to do.

This change presented itself as modern life. Men adapted, focusing on productivity, provision, and self-sufficiency, unaware that the very systems designed to increase comfort were also dissolving the conditions that once sustained a deep, consistent connection.

The result is the long-term outcome of cultural transition, a quiet inheritance passed down generation by generation, until many men find themselves living functional lives without the steady presence of a shared male community.

The Quiet Cost of Remote Work

Remote work didn't remove friendship outright. It removed the conditions that once made it effortless.

For many men, connection was never built through deliberate outreach or emotional planning. It formed through repetition, proximity, and shared time that didn't need to be scheduled. Coffee breaks. Passing conversations in hallways. Lunches that ran long. The casual decision to grab a drink after work because everyone was already there. None of these moments was profound on its own, yet together they created familiarity, trust, and continuity.

When work moved into screens and spare rooms, those moments disappeared quietly. Meetings became transactional. Conversations gained agendas. Interaction shrank to what was necessary, efficient, and contained within time slots. The informal spaces where relationships deepen, the unscripted minutes before and after work, the shared boredom and small talk that slowly turn colleagues into friends, were no longer part of the day.

What remained looked functional on the surface; tasks were completed, emails were answered, calendars stayed full, yet something essential was quietly missing. Without daily, low-stakes interaction, relationships stopped accumulating weight. There was no friction to soften distance and no shared rhythm to keep people close. So connection shifted into something that had to be initiated deliberately, a skill many men were never taught once proximity disappeared.

For men whose social lives revolved around work, this shift landed especially hard.

In many cases, coworkers weren't just professional contacts; they were the primary social circle. Work provided a steady stream of familiar faces, shared challenges, inside jokes, and mutual understanding. Over time, these relationships carried a sense of camaraderie that felt real, even if it rarely extended beyond office walls. When work went remote or hybrid, that entire ecosystem dissolved almost overnight.

The difference between work buddies and true friends became clearer once the shared space disappeared. Without daily proximity, many connections began to stall, messages slowed, group chats thinned out, and invitations quietly faded. What once felt solid revealed itself as situational, held together by an environment rather than depth. Men didn't lose friends through conflict or fallout; they lost the setting that had been carrying the relationship all along.

Relocation and the Reset of Belonging

Relocation compounds this loss in ways that are easy to underestimate. For example, think back to the first time you had to change schools. Even then, when life was simpler and responsibilities were lighter, the shift carried weight. Familiar faces disappeared. Routines broke. You had to relearn where you fit. That discomfort was your mind registering uncertainty. Change, by default, unsettles us.

As adults, the stakes are higher, and the margins are thinner. Moving cities for work, for stability, or for love doesn't just change geography; it disrupts identity. The brain is wired to seek familiarity and safety, and when environments shift abruptly, the amygdala, the part responsible for threat detection, becomes more active (Salzman, 2025). New places mean unknown rules, people, and outcomes. Even when the move is positive on paper, the body often interprets it as risk.

For men in their thirties and forties, this process feels fundamentally different than it once did. Social circles are more established, schedules are fuller, and energy is more carefully rationed. Friendship no longer forms automatically in school or early-career environments. Arriving in a new city as an adult often means starting from scratch, moving through unfamiliar spaces alone, and trying to build connections in places where everyone else already appears rooted and settled.

Relocation also separates men from the quiet support systems they rarely name. Friends who knew their history, habits, and blind spots are no longer nearby. The casual check-ins vanish. What remains is surface independence and underlying isolation. Many men adapt by focusing inward, telling themselves they'll rebuild later, once work stabilizes, or life slows down.

For some, the cost is heavier still. Leaving behind a spouse, children, or a familiar home to pursue work elsewhere introduces a different kind of strain. Physical distance stretches emotional connection. Guilt mixes with obligation. Loneliness intensifies in environments where success is expected, and vulnerability feels out of place. Over time, this combination can lead to persistent stress, emotional numbness, and depression that goes unspoken because it conflicts with the narrative of providing and progress.

None of this reflects personal weakness. It reflects a nervous system responding to sustained uncertainty without the buffering effect of a familiar community. When change stacks faster than the mind can form connections, the mind moves into protection mode. Energy narrows. Outreach slows. Isolation deepens, not as a choice, but as a response.

Understanding relocation this way matters. It reframes withdrawal as adaptation and loneliness as a signal, rather than a verdict. Men aren't failing to adjust; they are navigating repeated disruptions in a world that rarely gives them the time or structure to rebuild a sense of belonging before the next demand arrives.

Many men respond by withdrawing further. The effort required to meet new people feels disproportionate to the uncertain outcome. Rejection feels heavier, and awkwardness feels riskier, so they wait, telling themselves they'll figure it out later, while weeks and months pass without meaningful connection.

When Digital Connection Replaces Physical Presence

There's a quiet exhaustion that settles in when most of your interactions happen through screens.

At first, the digital connection feels efficient. Messages go out quickly. Group chats keep everyone loosely informed. Video calls put faces back into view. On the surface, it looks like a connection is still happening. Yet over time, something in the body begins to resist it.

After hours of staring at screens, talking on cue, and managing attention in virtual spaces, the appetite for more interaction drops. Not because men don't want connection, but because the form it comes in feels thin and demanding at the same time. The mind stays alert while the body remains alone. There's no shared silence, no physical presence, no sense of being together without performing.

Many men slip into what feels like ghost mode without intending to. Messages get read and answered later. Calls are postponed. Invitations sit unanswered, not out of disinterest, but out of depletion. Digital communication makes it easy to stay vaguely connected while slowly withdrawing from anything that requires energy you no longer have.

Group chats are a good example. They keep information circulating but rarely deepen the relationship. Updates replace stories. Reactions replace conversation. Everyone stays visible, yet no one feels particularly known. Over time, this creates a strange illusion of closeness without the substance that actually sustains friendship.

Video calls offer a similar tradeoff. You see faces but miss presence. You hear voices but lose the small cues that build trust, the pauses, the shared environment, the sense of occupying the same moment. When the call ends, the silence feels sharper because nothing was carried over.

None of this means digital tools are the enemy. They solve real problems and keep people in contact across distances. The cost appears when they become the primary or only form of connection. Without physical time together, friendship struggles to accumulate weight.

What looks like disengagement is often protection. The nervous system pulls back to conserve energy. Men don't stop caring. They stop initiating in environments that never quite give back what they require.

Understanding this changes the narrative. It explains why so many men feel socially drained despite constant communication, and why connection that lives only on screens rarely satisfies the deeper need to belong.

WHEN LIFE CHANGES

Then sometimes life simply moves you into a new season, and without realizing it, the shape of your days changes before your relationships have time to adjust.

Think about the first major transition you lived through. Maybe it was getting married. Maybe it was becoming a father. Maybe it was a breakup or a divorce that left everything familiar suddenly unstable. One chapter closed, another opened, and the space between those chapters felt lonelier than you expected.

Marriage often begins with expansion. There's love, commitment, and the building of something new. Time fills quickly with shared plans, responsibilities, and the quiet work of learning how to live alongside someone else. Without intention, friendships begin to prune themselves because attention narrows. Evenings once spent out become evenings in.

- Weekends reorganize around partnership.
- Messages get answered later.
- Invitations get postponed.

No one announces the shift, it just happens. Furthermore, fatherhood deepens this contraction. If you've become a dad, you know how suddenly your world rearranges itself. Sleep disappears, your energy thins, and suddenly, every spare moment is spoken for. The idea of meeting up feels heavier, not because you don't care, but because everything already feels full. Old friendships fade quietly under the weight of responsibility, and new ones don't automatically appear in their place.

Many new fathers look around and realize they don't know where friendships fit anymore. They search for other dads who understand the season they're in, yet often struggle to find spaces where those connections can form naturally. Conversations stay surface-level, and schedules rarely align. The isolation feels sharper because it arrives at a moment that's supposed to feel meaningful.

However, divorce or breakup introduces a different kind of loss.

When a long relationship ends, it often fractures a shared social world. Friends choose sides, drift away, or disappear into discomfort. Familiar gatherings stop happening. The sense of belonging you once felt evaporates alongside the relationship itself.

For many men, this is when loneliness lands hardest. The routines that once structured connections are gone, and rebuilding feels overwhelming at a moment when emotional reserves are already depleted.

- Reaching out feels risky.
- Starting again feels exhausting.
- Silence grows where support used to live.

These transitions tend to hit men differently. Furthermore, men are more likely to rely heavily on a partner for emotional and social support. When that support narrows or disappears, the absence is felt immediately. Friendships that were maintained casually now require effort and vulnerability, both of which can feel unfamiliar. While women often sustain connection through conversation and regular check-ins, many men were never taught to do friendship that way. When proximity disappears, so does the script.

None of this means you did something wrong. It means you moved through life stages that quietly reshaped your social world. It means the roles you stepped into demanded more of you than they gave back relationally. It means the structure that once supported friendship shifted faster than anyone prepared you for.

If you recognize yourself here, you're not alone, and you're not failing. You're responding to change the way most men do, by adapting, absorbing, and carrying on. The cost of that adaptation is distance. It's not because connection stopped mattering, but because no one ever showed you how to rebuild it when life moved on.

There's a reason rebuilding friendship as an adult feels harder than it looks, and it has less to do with effort and more to do with how you were taught to connect in the first place.

For most of your life, friendship didn't require much explanation. You bonded side by side, not face-to-face. You connected while doing something, not by talking about the connection itself. Work, sport, projects, shared struggle, these were the environments where trust formed naturally. A conversation happened, but it wasn't the entry point. It was the byproduct.

The Unspoken Rules of Male Friendship

Men are rarely explicitly taught the language of friendship. Instead, you learned a set of unspoken rules by watching and participating. You showed up, you did something together, you kept it light, and you didn't overanalyze. Closeness developed without needing to be named.

This works well when life provides shared spaces and repeated contact. It breaks down when those conditions disappear.

As an adult, you're often left trying to rebuild a connection without the environments that once carried it. There's no locker room, no shared shift, no automatic reason to be in the same place week after week. Without those structures, friendship begins to feel awkward, exposed, and unfamiliar.

At the same time, there's an unspoken pressure to appear self-sufficient. You're expected to handle your responsibilities quietly, manage stress internally, and avoid appearing needy. Wanting friendship can start to feel like admitting a deficiency, even though it's a basic human need.

So you hesitate. You second-guess reaching out. You worry about coming off as awkward, too eager, or out of place. You tell yourself everyone else already has their people, and you don't want to be the one forcing a connection where it doesn't belong.

Why Common Advice Misses the Mark

Much of the advice aimed at men misunderstands how male friendship actually works. Being told to "just open up" assumes that talking is the foundation of connection. For many men, it isn't. Depth often comes later, after trust is built through shared experience.

When advice skips that step, it creates pressure without structure. You're asked to be vulnerable without context, to share without safety, and to lead with emotion in environments that don't support it. No wonder it feels unnatural.

Previous generations had clearer models for male connection, not because men were better at friendship, but because the pathways were visible and unavoidable. Men gathered because life required it. They met in workshops and factories, on farms and docks, in union halls, churches, local clubs, barbershops, and neighborhood streets. They worked side by side, shared meals, argued, laughed, solved problems, and showed up again the next day. Friendship formed inside shared responsibility and repeated presence, not through planning, but through participation.

In those environments, belonging didn't need to be negotiated. You were known because you were seen regularly.

You earned trust by consistency, not disclosure. Over time, men learned each other's habits, strengths, weaknesses, and stories simply by living near one another and carrying weight together. Connection wasn't something you searched for, it was something you inherited through place, routine, and role.

As those spaces faded, very little rose to take their place. What disappeared wasn't just social venues, but the scaffolding that quietly held male friendship together. Without shared ground and repeated contact, connection lost its default setting and became something men were suddenly expected to create on their own, without a clear model for how.

What remains is a gap between desire and opportunity. You still want connection, but the blueprint that once guided it is missing. Without clear models, friendship begins to feel vague and uncertain, like something you're supposed to figure out instinctively but never quite learned how to do.

That uncertainty feeds a quiet pressure to fit an imagined standard. You begin measuring yourself against a narrow picture of what male friendship is supposed to look like: loud, effortless, built around sports, bars, or constant availability. When your life or temperament doesn't match that picture, it becomes easy to assume you're the exception rather than someone operating outside a flawed ideal.

The truth is simpler and more freeing: there has never been a single version of real friendship that men are meant to fit into. Some men connect through hiking, others through volunteering, gaming, faith, creative projects, or quiet routines shared over time. Age, background, culture, and temperament all shape how connections form and deepen.

The problem isn't that you don't fit the stereotype. The problem is that the stereotype was never the full picture. Understanding these differences matters because it shifts how you see yourself. It replaces self-criticism with clarity. It explains why rebuilding connection feels harder now, and why it doesn't have to stay that way once you understand the kind of friendship that actually fits your life.

However, there's a cost to drifting this far from connection, even when life looks stable on the outside.

You can function for a long time without naming it. You go to work, you show up for your family, you keep moving. From the outside, nothing looks broken. Inside, something slowly tightens. The weight doesn't come from a single moment; it builds from the absence of places where you can be fully known without performing.

Health Effects of Loneliness

Loneliness doesn't stay neatly contained in the social part of your life. It leaks into the body.

Men who lack close, consistent friendships experience higher levels of chronic stress. Without trusted peers to process life alongside, tension stays internal. Over time, that stress shows up as irritability, fatigue, anxiety, or a low-grade heaviness that never quite lifts. Many men don't label this as loneliness. They call it pressure, burnout, or just being tired all the time.

Left unaddressed, isolation is linked to depression, substance use, and physical health problems that shorten life expectancy, and the pathway is well understood. When connection thins, stress stops being processed socially and stays trapped inside the body. Cortisol levels remain elevated for longer periods. Inflammation increases. The nervous system remains in a low-grade state of alert rather than returning to baseline.

Over time, this chronic stress response begins to wear systems down.

1. Heart health suffers as blood pressure rises and recovery slows.
2. Sleep degrades because the mind never fully stands down at night.
3. The immune system weakens, making illness linger longer and healing take more time.
4. Energy drops not because you're lazy, but because your body is operating without relief.

Social connection acts as a regulator. Being around people you trust lowers stress hormones, stabilizes mood, and signals safety to the brain. Without that regulation, many men turn to substitutes that offer short-term relief: alcohol, overwork, numbing routines, anything that quiets the pressure temporarily. These coping mechanisms don't create recovery, they delay it, often at a long-term cost.

The body was never designed to carry everything alone. Humans evolved to process threat, effort, and emotion in groups, not in isolation. When men shoulder stress privately for years, the load embeds itself physically, quietly shaping health outcomes long before anything feels dramatic enough to name.

When friendship outside the home thins, pressure concentrates inward. Partners often become the sole outlet for emotional processing, stress relief, and social connection. That's a heavy load for any relationship to carry. Without realizing it, you may begin asking one person to meet needs that were once distributed across a wider circle.

Over time, this imbalance can strain even strong marriages. Conversations feel heavier, and tension lingers longer. Small conflicts carry more weight because there's nowhere else to release pressure. The absence of outside support doesn't stay outside; it moves into the home.

Fatherhood and Emotional Availability

Fatherhood adds meaning and responsibility, but it also narrows the margin. When you're isolated, showing up emotionally for your children becomes harder because emotional reserves are already depleted. Patience runs thinner, and presence becomes harder to sustain. Kids don't need perfect fathers, they need regulated ones, and regulation is difficult without support.

Men with strong friendships often parent differently, not because they're better fathers, but because they're less alone. They have spaces to offload stress, gain perspective, and remember who they are outside of their role.

Isolation also reshapes how you show up professionally, often in ways that are easy to miss at first. Without trusted peers to think out loud with, challenges begin to feel heavier, and setbacks land more personally. Motivation dulls, creativity narrows, and resilience drops, not because your standards changed, but because you're carrying pressure alone.

Men with meaningful friendships tend to perform better at work, not because friendship replaces ambition, but because it reinforces identity and confidence. When you're supported, effort feels shared, perspective widens, and work stops feeling like a solitary test of your worth.

When you're connected, you take healthier risks and recover faster from failure. You don't carry every outcome as a referendum on your worth.

However, none of these effects arrives suddenly. They accumulate quietly, disguised as normal adulthood. The danger is endurance without support. Friendship is part of the infrastructure that keeps you mentally steady, emotionally available, and physically well. When that infrastructure erodes, everything else carries more weight.

Understanding the cost clarifies what's at stake. Connection functions as protection. It steadies your health, strengthens your relationships, and supports the life you're carrying forward. When friendship is present, the weight of life is distributed. When it's absent, everything else grows heavier.

KEY TAKEAWAYS

- Loneliness rarely arrives through failure or conflict. It forms through structural change, shifting seasons, and the quiet removal of spaces where connection once happened naturally.

- Modern life reduced proximity, repetition, and shared environments, the very conditions that sustained male friendship for generations.

- Major life transitions, such as marriage, fatherhood, relocation, and loss, narrow social circles unless new structures replace the old ones.

- Men build connection differently, often side by side, through shared activity and consistency rather than immediate emotional disclosure.

- Isolation carries real consequences for health, relationships, parenting, work, and identity, even when life appears stable on the surface.

- Friendship functions as infrastructure. When it weakens, pressure concentrates elsewhere.

The patterns are clearer now. What you've been feeling unfolded through a sequence of changes, structures shifted, environments rearranged, roles expanded, and connections gradually thinned. None of that makes you deficient. It reflects what happens when human needs outpace systems that no longer teach or support the rebuilding of connection.

Clarity changes posture. When you can name what happened, you stop fighting yourself and start orienting forward. The question isn't whether connection matters. The question is how it actually forms, how it survives change, and how it can be rebuilt deliberately within the life you're already living. That's where the work turns practical. From here, the focus shifts to structure and understanding how real friendships take shape over time.

CHAPTER 2:
WHEN FRIENDSHIP STOPS BEING AUTOMATIC

"We do not remember days, we remember moments." - Cesare Pavese

There are seasons in life when something feels off, even though nothing looks wrong. You wake up, handle your responsibilities, get through the day, and keep things moving. From the outside, life appears stable. Inside, there's a quiet sense of distance that's hard to explain. Not pain exactly, but more like absence. A missing layer you can't quite point to without sounding dramatic.

This experience shows up when life changes faster than connection can keep up. When routines shift, roles expand, and the spaces where friendship once lived quietly disappear.

Before we talk about structure or systems, it matters to pause here because what you're carrying has been carried by others, often in silence, and also often with the same questions running underneath. What follows is a series of ordinary moments that slowly added up, moments you're likely to recognize without needing much explanation at all.

Moving Without Realizing What You Lost

There's a point after a move when the novelty wears off. At first, everything feels manageable. The decision made sense, the job pays better, the schedule is flexible, and the location feels like progress. You unpack, settle in, and tell yourself you'll find your rhythm soon.

Days fill up easily as work takes most of your focus, and evenings slip into familiar routines. You keep in touch with people from before through messages and group chats. You're close enough to feel connected, yet distant enough that reaching further can always wait until later.

Then time stretches.

Weeks pass without anyone really knowing how your days look now. There's no one to grab coffee with on impulse, no familiar face you run into without planning, no shared context carrying conversation forward. Every interaction suddenly requires intention, and intention feels heavier than you expected.

You don't call it loneliness. You tell yourself you enjoy the quiet. You say you're busy. You assume this is just what happens when you grow up. Still, some moments land differently. Laughing alone at something you would've shared. Sitting with a thought longer than necessary. Realizing no one nearby would notice if your week was heavier than usual.

Nothing fell apart. No friendships ended badly. What changed was proximity.

The structure that once made connections effortless is gone, and no one teaches you how to replace it. Not because you failed, but because this is the first time friendship requires deliberate building instead of shared circumstance.

If this feels familiar, it's probably because it's a common turning point many men pass through without a name for it.

When Your World Shrinks After Becoming a Father

No one really prepares you for how quickly your time disappears.

At first, the days blur together. Sleep comes in pieces. Your attention is constantly pulled outward, toward needs that can't wait. You love your child deeply, and that love reorganizes everything. What surprises you is how completely it consumes the space where friendship once lived.

You still think about reaching out. You still care. It just never feels like the right moment. Evenings that once held flexibility now hold exhaustion. Weekends fill with responsibility before they ever open up. Making plans feels like committing energy you're not sure you'll have when the time comes.

Sometimes friends don't disappear all at once; things simply begin to change. Some people stop reaching out because they don't know what to say; others feel caught in the middle and quietly pull back. Invitations slow, group dynamics shift, and you start noticing the gaps before you can fully explain them.

You keep functioning, handling logistics, and continuing to show up where you're supposed to, doing what needs to be done. From the outside, it looks like an adjustment, but underneath, there's a sense of standing in unfamiliar territory without a map.

Reaching out feels heavier now because vulnerability carries more risk when you're already exposed. Some days you want company, while other days you want to be left alone until things feel steadier, and both impulses can exist at the same time without canceling each other out.

This kind of loneliness has a different texture. It's tied to grief, to the quiet work of letting go, to rebuilding identity one piece at a time. You're not just looking for new friends, you're figuring out who you are in a life that doesn't look the way it used to.

Nothing about this means you're falling behind. It means you're standing in a transition that reshaped more than one relationship at once.

Finding Your Place Outside the Expected Mold

At some point, you may have realized you never fully fit the version of friendship you saw growing up. You weren't drawn to the loudest rooms or the most obvious social spaces. You enjoyed connection, just not in the ways that seemed most celebrated. That difference often went unnoticed when life provided structure. It becomes harder to ignore once you're responsible for building connections yourself.

- You hesitate before joining anything new.
- You wonder if you'll belong.
- You worry about sticking out or needing to explain yourself.

The pressure to match an unspoken standard makes retreat feel safer than trying. Sometimes, almost without planning, you come across a space that fits. A hobby, a routine, or a shared interest gives you a reason to show up regularly. You're doing something alongside others, and conversation starts moving on its own because there's shared ground holding it up. Familiarity builds through repetition, and trust takes shape quietly, without being forced.

The relief arrives without announcement. You begin to feel more settled in yourself as the days find a steadier rhythm. The shift comes from being in an environment that aligns with how you connect, where showing up feels natural rather than performative.

These experiences differ in detail, but they carry the same undercurrent. Connection faded not through failure, but through change. Each narrative turns on a small realization: the problem wasn't effort or personality, it was the absence of structure.

Seeing that pattern brings relief. What once felt scattered begins to make sense. The experience gains shape and meaning.

As these stories settle, a few familiar thoughts rise to the surface:

- It feels like everyone else already has their group.
- It feels like a window closed without warning.

- It feels like the version of friendship you were taught to expect never quite fit.

Those thoughts grow from comparison without context. You're measuring outcomes without seeing the structure beneath them. Every man you've just met showed up with effort, care, and intention. The difference came down to whether a framework existed that matched the season he was living in.

The real movement happens in small turning points. For instance:

- When proximity becomes visible as the engine of connection.
- When responsibility is seen clearly as outpacing support.
- When belonging comes into focus through environment rather than self-reinvention.

These moments shift direction and transform uncertainty into orientation.

From here, attention turns to understanding how friendship forms in real life, how it endures through change, and how it can be deliberately rebuilt with the time, energy, and life you already carry.

How Adult Male Friendship Forms

Connection takes time to cultivate. It takes shape through time spent in the same places, through faces that become familiar, and through moments that repeat often enough to feel safe.

Long before trust becomes personal, your system looks for consistency. It notices who shows up, who belongs in the same environment, and who feels predictable rather than surprising.

1. Familiarity opens the door.

2. Safety settles in next.

3. Meaning develops later.

This sequence plays out quietly, often without you noticing. You feel it when conversation starts flowing with less effort, when silence feels easier to share, when presence stops feeling performative and starts feeling natural.

You've seen this pattern play out across your life. At the gym, where the same faces become part of your routine. At work, where shared projects create an unspoken understanding. In faith spaces, hobbies, neighborhoods, and seasons, where repeated proximity turns strangers into known quantities. Over time, shared experience carries more weight than any single conversation.

This is how the mind builds trust. Repetition calms the nervous system because predictability creates ease. Shared context allows connection to deepen without being forced. Friendship grows because these conditions accumulate, not because anyone tries to make something happen too quickly.

What follows gives language to that lived process. It helps you recognize where connection stands, how it progresses, and why certain moments feel natural while others feel premature. With clarity, you move forward with awareness instead of guessing.

Stage One: First Contact

This stage is simple; you meet someone in a repeated environment. Could be the gym, at work, at perhaps church, maybe a run club, or just the same coffee spot at the same hour. You don't sit down and pour out your life story; you barely talk at all.

It's a nod. A "what's up." A quick comment about the workout, the meeting, the weather. You see each other again next week. Then the week after.

What's happening here is neurological. Your brain is registering familiarity. Safety starts forming through repetition. This is why showing up matters more than saying something impressive. A lot of guys sabotage this stage by trying to be interesting instead of consistent. You don't need charisma here; your presence alone is enough, so just keep showing up.

If you've ever thought, "I see this guy all the time, but we never really talk," congratulations. You're exactly where you're supposed to be.

Stage Two: Acquaintances — Small Talk

Now the ice thaws a bit. Conversations last longer than thirty seconds.

1. You exchange names properly.
2. You learn what he does.
3. Where he trains.
4. What days he usually comes in.

This stage answers one quiet question: does this feel comfortable? Also, take it slow and easy here because you need to understand the person you're dealing with first. You don't want to paint the wrong perspective and have your intentions misinterpreted. The key is to always get to know the person from a distance before approaching them.

So at this point, you're paying attention to energy.

- Does conversation flow or feel forced?
- Does he ask back when you ask him something?
- Do you both smile and move on without awkwardness?

This stage can take weeks, sometimes months, even, but that's actually pretty normal. Just don't rush it.

A common mistake here is trying to turn an acquaintance into a best friend overnight. Another is overthinking silence. Ease is the signal; let it do its work.

Most adult friendships stall or grow right here. Guys either wait forever for the other person to make a move, or they push too hard. A simple move works best.

- "I'm grabbing coffee after this."
- "We usually lift on Tuesdays."

Low pressure, but the rhythm is very clear.

You don't need deep talks yet. Shared experience is doing the heavy lifting. Stories accumulate naturally, context builds, and you just relax around each other.

This is where things start feeling real because you're no longer running into each other by accident. You come at the same time, you sometimes train together, you grab a coffee afterward, or you expect to see each other. This stage builds trust through rhythm.

Stage Three: Regulars — Shared Rhythm

This is where things start feeling real. You're no longer running into each other by accident; you come at the same time. You train together sometimes. You grab a coffee after. You expect to see each other.

This stage builds trust through rhythm. You show up, do the thing together, and let shared experience carry the weight. Stories accumulate naturally, context builds effortlessly, and over time, you find yourself relaxing around each other.

Most adult friendships stall or grow right here. Guys either wait forever for the other person to make a move, or they push too hard. A simple move works best. "I'm grabbing coffee after this." "We usually lift on Tuesdays." Low pressure. Clear rhythm.

Stage Four: Buddies — Mutual Investment

At this point, effort balances. You text without a reason, and plans extend beyond the original setting. You talk about real life, not just the activity that brought you together.

This stage is when friendship starts to feel dependable. You show up for each other in small ways, such as offering advice, offering support, or just checking in. You don't wonder where you stand.

This stage requires adaptation. When work shifts or schedules change, new rhythms replace old ones. Friendship endures when it evolves alongside life.

Stage Five: Trusted Crew — Solid Ground

This stage forms over time, often without announcement.

- Years pass.
- Life shifts.
- Jobs change.
- Families grow.
- Schedules tighten.

Through all of that, a few connections remain steady. You don't talk every day, sometimes weeks or even months go by, but when you reconnect, it feels intact and so authentic, like there was never any silence whatsoever.

Such a trusted crew is built on shared history. You've seen each other in different seasons, and you know each other's patterns, strengths, blind spots, and limits. You understand how the other person handles stress, success, and disappointment. Silence feels comfortable because nothing needs to be proven.

Reliability defines this stage. You trust these men to show up when it matters because support moves both ways without scorekeeping. Advice carries weight because it comes from context, not opinion. You don't need to pretend here, just come as you are with all your strengths and weaknesses.

This level of friendship holds through distance and change because it isn't dependent on constant contact. It's anchored in trust built over time and reinforced through shared experience.

Most men have a small number of relationships at this level. That concentration is natural. Depth gathers where time and consistency allow it. Essentially, a trusted crew steadies your life.

So seeing the pattern brings relief. When you recognize how connection grows, expectations settle. You understand why depth takes time, why certain moments arrive later, and why progress feels steady rather than instant. The tension around timing fades, replaced by clarity about where you are and what fits next. Friendship becomes something you build with intention, patience, and rhythm, inside the life you already have.

Furthermore, understanding how friendship forms doesn't solve everything, but it removes the confusion that keeps you stuck. From here, the work isn't about forcing connection, it's about learning how to read what's already unfolding

CHAPTER 3:
DISCERNMENT

"Patience is not passive; it is concentrated strength." - Bruce Lee

At this point, the work shifts from understanding friendship to reading it. You already know that connection grows through time, rhythm, and shared presence. What matters now is learning how to recognize what's actually happening in front of you, without forcing momentum or second-guessing every interaction. Most friendships don't stall loudly, they slow through small signals. You start noticing who follows through, who initiates back, and where energy naturally meets you halfway. Plans either settle into something expected or stay vague. Conversation either carries forward or resets every time. Paying attention here changes everything.

When effort is mutual, leaning in feels natural.

- A simple invitation lands easily.
- Time together starts arranging itself without friction.

- You don't feel the need to push because momentum already exists.

When effort stays one-sided, clarity matters more than persistence. Repeatedly carrying the weight of initiation usually means alignment hasn't formed. That information saves you energy and helps you place your effort where it can actually grow.

There are moments when holding steady is the right move.

- Letting rhythm develop.
- Allowing familiarity to deepen.
- Giving connection room to mature without pressure.

There are also moments when letting a connection be what it is becomes an act of respect, for yourself and the other person. Not every interaction is meant to move forward, and discernment protects you from chasing outcomes that don't fit. This doesn't necessarily mean you should start doing less than you already were, it just means assess and adjust accordingly and accurately.

As you learn to read these signals, friendship stops feeling confusing or unpredictable. You gain a sense of when to lean in, when to hold your pace, and when to redirect your energy.

From here, that awareness deepens. You start noticing the imbalance sooner, adjust before frustration sets in, and keep your energy aligned with the kind of connection you want to grow.

READING THE WARNING SIGNS

There's a point where effort stops being growth and starts becoming strain. You don't always notice it right away. At first, you tell yourself it's just timing, perhaps schedules clash, or life gets busy. You give it space, and that's actually reasonable, but over time, patterns begin to repeat, and patterns are what matter here.

When Effort Stops Moving Both Ways: One of the clearest signals shows up in initiation. If you're always the one suggesting plans, checking in, or keeping the thread alive, pay attention to how that feels in your body. Not frustration in a dramatic sense, but a quiet heaviness. The sense that you're carrying something that used to feel shared. A healthy connection has movement in both directions. It doesn't have to be equal every week, but over time, there's a balance. When effort keeps flowing in one direction, momentum naturally drains.

When Plans Stay Vague: Another signal shows up in how plans land. You suggest something simple. The response sounds friendly, but nothing ever quite solidifies. "We should do that sometime." "Yeah, let's see." Time passes, and the idea floats without ever touching ground. Clarity builds connection, whilst vagueness keeps it suspended. When a friendship is ready to move forward, plans tend to find form. Times get named, and patterns emerge. When that doesn't happen repeatedly, it's worth noticing without trying to push things into place.

When Energy Feels Contained: Sometimes connection stays boxed into a single setting. You talk easily at work, at the gym, or during an activity, but it never extends beyond that environment. Conversation resets each time, staying pleasant but surface-level. This isn't inherently negative because some connections are meant to live exactly where they are. The signal appears when you try to extend the environment slightly and feel resistance or indifference.

When You Feel the Urge to Compensate: A subtle warning sign often shows up internally. You start thinking about what else you could do.

- Say something deeper.
- Be more interesting.
- Offer more.
- Adjust yourself to keep the connection alive.

That urge usually means alignment hasn't formed yet. Real friendship doesn't require constant compensation. It grows through shared presence, not performance or pretense.

Patience, Discernment, and Reading the Pattern

Not every signal asks for movement. Sometimes the strongest response is patience, letting rhythm settle, giving familiarity the space to deepen at its own pace. Consistency has a way of doing quiet work over time, especially when pressure stays low and expectations remain grounded. You can usually feel the difference.

- Growth carries a sense of space.

- Conversation flows without effort.
- Time together feels easy to return to.
- Strain feels tighter.
- You notice yourself thinking more about what to do next, how to adjust, how to keep things alive.

There are also moments when allowing a connection to remain exactly where it is becomes the wisest choice. Some relationships live comfortably within a shared setting or activity. They add texture to your life without asking to become something deeper. Letting them stay light preserves energy for the connections that have room to grow. This kind of discernment comes from stepping back and looking at patterns rather than isolated moments. You start noticing who meets effort with effort, where plans take shape naturally, and where presence feels mutual rather than managed. Over time, these patterns make it clear where to invest and where to ease off.

As that awareness settles in, friendship stops feeling unpredictable. You respond to what's unfolding instead of trying to manufacture outcomes. Your energy stays aligned with the connections that can actually sustain it. Your social world begins to organize itself with less friction and more clarity.

BUILDING FRIENDSHIP

There's a quiet expectation many men carry without realizing it. You meet someone, then immediately, conversation clicks, you laugh easily, and you just conclude that there's chemistry.

Somewhere underneath that moment, a question forms: *Is this one of my guys?*

That question is actually accurate, but then the problem is the timeline attached to it. Most of us absorbed our model of friendship early, when connections formed fast. School did the work for us. Proximity was automatic, and time was abundant. Friendship felt immediate because the structure carried it. However, Adulthood works differently. Instead of instant depth, friendship now grows by accumulation. Time on the graph matters more than intensity at the start.

Imagine friendship as a curve rather than a switch. At the beginning, progress is slow. You invest time, show up, share space, and very little seems to happen. Then something subtle shifts. Recognition turns into familiarity. Familiarity into rhythm. Rhythm into trust. Over time, the curve steepens and the depth increases because history supports it.

The mistake many men make is expecting the curve to spike early. When that spike doesn't come, doubt creeps in. You start wondering if the connection is weak, if you missed the window, if something is wrong with how you relate. In reality, the curve is simply doing what it's designed to do.

A useful way to picture this is a simple pie. At first, most of the circle is made up of shared activity and presence. Time spent together doing something side by side. Conversation stays light because it doesn't need to carry weight yet. As months pass, another slice grows. Personal context, shared stories, and trust built through consistency. Much later, a smaller but meaningful slice appears. Vulnerability, advice, and support that only work because the other pieces already exist.

Trying to flip that order collapses the structure. Deep disclosure without shared history feels heavy. Intensity without rhythm feels unstable. What looks like confidence can feel like pressure on the receiving end.

Strong friendships rarely announce themselves. They sneak up on you, then one day you realize you trust someone's opinion. Another day, you notice you're relaxed around them. Later still, you recognize that they are steadily part of your life.

This is why comparison causes so much frustration. You're seeing other men at the top of the curve without witnessing the long, quiet stretch at the bottom. You're comparing someone else's accumulated years to your first few interactions. When you let go of the instant-best-friend expectation, something loosens.

- You stop auditioning people.
- You stop pressuring moments to mean more than they're ready to mean.
- You allow connection to grow at the speed it can sustain.

Friendship becomes less about finding the right person quickly and more about staying present long enough for the right depth to emerge. That shift changes how you move forward; you stop chasing and start building conditions, and that's where the real work begins.

BUDDY AUDIT

Before building anything new, it helps to understand what already exists. Most men carry a sense of their social world without ever really seeing it. Connections overlap, drift, resurface, and fade, all without being named. When everything stays undefined, action feels heavier than it needs to be.

So this part begins with orientation. Think about the people already present in your life. Some sit close, others live on the edges. Some belong to a specific season or setting, others remain connected mostly through screens or memory. Until you slow down and notice where people actually stand, everything blends.

Imagine your social world as a loose landscape rather than a fixed diagram. At the center are the people you trust and feel at ease with. Conversation flows without preparation, and context is shared. These are the relationships that ground you. Beyond that center are people you see with some regularity.

- Work connections.
- Gym regulars.
- Neighbors.
- Hobby partners.

Time together feels familiar even if depth is still forming. Further out are situational connections such as group chats and online communities. Essentially, these are friends you enjoy but rarely see. These relationships still matter; they simply play a different role.

Some connections once sat closer and now live further out, shaped by time, shifting routines, and the natural rearranging of life. As you look across this landscape, notice where most of your connections live. If nearly everything runs through one environment, that's useful information. If most support flows through one person, often a partner, that matters too. Narrow foundations can feel stable until pressure hits. This is also where overlooked opportunities show up. Think about the people who almost fit.

- The coworker you always talk to but never see outside work.
- The gym regular you joke with.
- The old friend who crosses your mind now and then.

These connections often sit closer than they appear. Turning one of these into something more usually comes from a small extension of the existing environment.

- A shared coffee.
- A follow-up message.
- An invitation that feels natural rather than forced.

This will help you to evaluate and address your interactions accordingly without forcing any outcomes. When you can name where people stand, decisions simplify. You know where to invest, where to expand, and where to leave things as they are. Of course, this view may change over time due to factors such as schedule adjustments. But should that happen, you can always return to this perspective and reevaluate. However, for now, clarity is enough. Once you can see your social world as it stands, your next steps begin to feel grounded rather than abstract.

Momentum, Direction, And Small Wins

Friendship grows through attention more than effort. By this point, you've already seen how connections form, how they deepen, and how they stall. What matters now is learning how to stay oriented once movement begins, without turning friendship into a project or losing its natural feel.

Knowing When Something Is Moving: Progress often announces itself quietly. A conversation carries forward instead of restarting from scratch. Seeing each other starts feeling expected rather than coincidental. An invitation lands easily and turns into an actual plan. You don't overthink whether reaching out will feel awkward. Those are signals, and they tell you that the connection has enough footing to hold a little more weight. Not more intensity, just a small extension of what already exists. Most friendships grow this way, by adding inches rather than making leaps.

Choosing Direction That Fits Your Life: Clarity changes how you invest your energy. Instead of trying to deepen every connection, you start asking a simpler question: what kind of connection would support this season of my life? For some men, that means one or two people they can consistently see at an activity they enjoy. For others, it looks like a small group that understands limited time and shifting schedules. Direction works like a filter; it keeps you from chasing everything and helps you recognize what actually fits. When direction is clear, effort feels lighter. You invest where alignment already exists, rather than forcing momentum where it doesn't.

Noticing Progress Without Overthinking It: Friendship builds confidence through evidence. You notice:

- When you follow through.
- When you show up.
- When you extend an invitation and receive a clear response.

These moments matter because they show movement, even when the outcome stays modest. Paying attention to these small shifts keeps you grounded. You stay encouraged without needing dramatic results. Progress becomes something you recognize, not something you wait for.

Staying Flexible as Life Shifts: Connection grows inside real life, not around it. Schedules change, energy fluctuates, availability expands and contracts, some friendships deepen faster than expected, and others settle into a steady place and hold there for a while. Flexibility allows connection to breathe. You respond to what the season allows instead of pushing past it. When something flows, you protect it. When something tightens, you reassess and adjust your focus. Friendship strengthens when it's given room to evolve naturally.

As you move forward with this awareness, the system becomes personal. You shape it around your personality, your time, and the way you naturally connect, rather than following a rigid formula.

Taking Ownership

You've covered a lot of ground and hopefully gained some insight as well. So take some time to reflect on these questions:

- When you imagine your social world six months from now, what feels missing right now?
- Where does connection already feel easy, even if it hasn't gone very deep yet?
- Which environments bring out the most natural version of you?
- Who comes to mind when you think about shared rhythm rather than shared history?
- What kind of support would actually make this season of life feel steadier?

Your answers will become patterns that will guide you as you move forward. Also, you don't need to build friendship the same way anyone else does. Some men connect best one-on-one, through routine and familiarity, whilst others thrive in small groups built around activity or purpose. Some prefer quieter rhythms, others enjoy hosting and bringing people together. Pay attention to what energizes you rather than what you think should work.

This system adapts to your personality, schedule, and capacity. You're allowed to skip steps, revisit earlier ideas, or stay longer where something feels alive.

A small exercise for you this week:

The Monday Playbook

Keep this simple. This is a weekly check-in. At the start of the week, choose one of the following:

- Reach out to one person you already see or talk to regularly.
- Extend an interaction slightly, coffee after, a short walk, a follow-up message.
- Show up to something you've been considering but haven't acted on yet.

That's the move for the week.

At the end of the week, pause for a moment and notice:

- What felt easy?
- What surprised you?
- What felt worth repeating?

CHAPTER 4:
INITIATION WITHOUT PRESSURE

"Be tolerant with others and strict with yourself." - Marcus Aurelius

Connection rarely announces itself. It starts quietly, with awareness, with noticing who's already there and how the space feels before anything is said. You're already sharing space with people every day, in rooms, routines, and stretches of time that repeat just enough to feel familiar. What changes things isn't confidence turned up loud, it's attention tuned correctly. Noticing what's already there, then extending yourself a few inches into it.

The tension most men feel around starting something new isn't a result of a lack of social skill; it actually comes from the pressure to make the moment mean more than it needs to. When the goal shrinks, when the reach stays light, the body relaxes. Conversation finds its own pace, and silence stops feeling like a problem to solve.

Connection grows best when it's allowed to breathe. You read the room before you step into it. You match the energy instead of trying to override it. You offer an opening and leave space for it to be taken or left without consequence.

That's the posture here. Small extensions, clear signals, no performance required.

From that footing, initiation settles into something simpler and more natural. Not effortless, but grounded. A way of moving toward people that keeps you steady regardless of what comes back.

READING THE ROOM

You can feel it before you name it. The room has a tempo. Sometimes it's open and loose, sometimes contained and inward. People broadcast far more than they realize through posture, pacing, and attention. Someone lingering after an activity instead of rushing out. A glance that returns instead of sliding past. A half-smile that stays when you speak. These are cues to observe or pay attention to.

Reading the room starts with slowing your own movement. When you arrive already charged, everything looks like a green light or a rejection. When you arrive steadily, information becomes clearer. You take in who's settled and who's guarded. You notice whether the conversation is spilling outward or staying tight to its corners. You don't force yourself into the center, but you let the environment tell you where you fit.

Think about a crowded coffee shop versus a quiet co-working space. In one, energy is shared, and quick comments pass easily between strangers. In the other, focus is protected, and interruptions land heavier. Same people, different rules. Matching the setting is a form of respect. It signals awareness before words ever do.

Sometimes the invitation is obvious. A body stays open as you approach, shoulders angle toward you instead of away, and the exchange stretches a few seconds longer than necessary. At other times, the signal is restrained. Headphones remain in, eyes stay down, replies close rather than open. That isn't a failure, it's information. Letting it register without tightening or pushing is part of staying grounded.

The easiest openings grow out of what's already there, a sticker on a laptop that hints at a shared interest, a book you recognize, a piece of gear you've been curious about. Simple observations keep the exchange light because they don't ask for anything in return. Often, a nod and a single sentence are enough. When it moves, you stay with it. When it doesn't, you step away cleanly.

There's strength in knowing when to exit as well. Leaving a moment intact preserves dignity on both sides, a quick smile, a short sign-off, a clean step away. You don't owe an explanation, and you don't need to rescue the silence. Humor can help when it fits, but clarity carries just as much weight. You leave without collapsing inward or compensating outward.

Over time, this way of moving builds trust in yourself. You learn that approach isn't a test of worth, it's a check for alignment. You gather small confirmations instead of chasing big reactions. That steadiness keeps you available for the moments that are ready to meet you halfway.

Extending the Thread

When those moments arrive, when the exchange feels easy, and the energy doesn't collapse, the question quietly shifts from whether connection is possible to how it continues. Nothing dramatic changes, there's no clear signal to act, just a sense that something could carry forward if it's handled with care.

Momentum rarely comes from a big move. It comes from a small extension that lands easily and leaves room on both sides. A moment turns into something more, not because it's pushed forward, but because it's invited.

This is where many men tighten up without realizing it. The interaction felt good, so the instinct is to lock it down, define it, or make it mean something immediately. That impulse is understandable, but it usually does the opposite of what you want. Connection stays alive when it's given space to choose its next step.

Think of an extension as a thread you place gently on the table. It's visible, available, and easy to pick up, but it doesn't demand attention. When someone reaches for it, you feel it right away. When they don't, nothing breaks.

Some extensions happen in the moment.

- *"I'm heading out for a bit after this."*
- *"I'm usually around here midweek."*
- *"A couple of us tend to hang back for a while."*

These lines simply open a door and let the other person decide whether to step through. Nothing needs to be explained, clarified, or followed up on. The lightness works because there's no outcome to manage, only space being offered.

Other extensions travel through a screen.

Sometimes a message makes more sense than an in-person ask, especially when routines are tight or energy is low. Digital-first outreach isn't avoidance, it's adaptation. The same principles apply.

Keep it short.

Keep it human.

Leave space.

- *"Good meeting you earlier. If you're ever up for coffee, let me know."*
- *"Saw this and thought of our convo."*
- *"A few of us are doing trivia this week, feel free to join."*

Notice the tone here. Nothing is locked in or chased, and the message stands comfortably on its own without needing a response to feel complete.

Group settings help here. Inviting someone into something that already exists lowers the social weight for everyone involved. It signals inclusion without creating a one-on-one obligation. If it fits, it fits. If it doesn't, the rhythm stays intact.

Timing matters more than cleverness. An extension offered while things feel easy lands differently than one dropped after weeks of silence. When momentum is present, even small gestures feel natural. When it isn't, restraint protects your footing. Sometimes the thread isn't picked up right away, and messages go unanswered, or schedules don't align. That space doesn't need to be filled or explained away. Silence is often just silence, not feedback or rejection, and allowing it to remain neutral keeps you available for whatever comes next.

Extending the thread is a skill that strengthens with repetition. Each time you offer something without overinvesting, you reinforce a steady posture. You learn that movement doesn't require certainty, only willingness. Over time, those small extensions begin to gather into something real, not because they were forced, but because they were allowed to find their place.

When that extension is met, even briefly, the moment shifts again. Now you're no longer testing whether a connection is possible; you're simply sharing a few minutes of space. What matters here isn't momentum or depth, but staying present without rushing the exchange.

Conversation doesn't need to be carried on, it just needs to be allowed. The pressure to keep things moving usually arises when someone starts reaching ahead of the moment instead of staying in it. Ease shows up when attention stays anchored in what's already shared.

Over time, you stop measuring conversations by length or outcome and start noticing feel. Whether presence was mutual or perhaps the exchange carried itself. That awareness keeps you relaxed in the moment and makes the next extension, when it comes, feel natural rather than forced.

Non-Awkward Conversation Starters

Sometimes the moment is there, but the words don't show up on time. When that happens, it helps to have a few natural starting points that fit different settings and personalities. They work because they fit the moment, not because they're clever or rehearsed.

Event-based

Events already give you a shared reason to be there, so you don't need to manufacture interest. Pay attention to the energy of the space, keep it situational, and let humor stay subtle. Public settings reward awareness more than boldness.

- *"How'd you find out about this?"*
- *"You been to one of these before?"*
- *"What made you come out tonight?"*

Shared interest

When someone brings something into a space, a book, gear, music, or a game, they've already given you an opening. Responding to what they chose keeps the exchange natural and removes the pressure to be creative.

- *"I noticed your D&D dice. What campaign are you running?"*
- *"That setup looks solid, how long you been using it?"*
- *"You into that band or did it just come on?"*

Environment-based

This works best when you comment on what you are both already experiencing. Music, atmosphere, waiting, the flow of the place. Neutral observations make it easy for the other person to engage or opt out without awkwardness.

- *"This playlist's better than I expected."*
- *"That's a solid book, what do you think so far?"*
- *"This place always this busy?"*

Soft starts (low pressure)

These are especially useful if you're more reserved or just not in the mood to perform. Practical questions lower the emotional weight and give the interaction a clear, natural shape.

- *"Quick question, do you know a good coffee spot around here?"*
- *"I just moved here, still figuring things out."*
- *"I don't usually come to stuff like this, but it looked interesting."*

When the conversation stalls

Not every exchange is meant to stretch. When energy dips, closing cleanly preserves the interaction and keeps things human. Ease matters more than continuity here.

- *"Anyway, didn't mean to interrupt, good luck with it."*
- *"I'll let you get back to it."*
- *"Good seeing you."*

Leaving a light bridge

Only use these when the interaction already feels comfortable. Think of them as leaving a door unlocked rather than asking someone to walk through it immediately.

- *"If you ever want to join trivia night, let me know."*
- *"We should compare notes on hiking spots sometime."*
- *"We're usually around here midweek."*

What matters is fit, not polish. An opener that matches the moment gives the other person room to respond naturally. That's how most connections begin, not with cleverness, but with ease and space for the exchange to unfold on its own.

TEXTING

Texting amplifies energy. Whatever state you're in when you hit send tends to show up louder on the other side of the screen. Calm reads calm, and curious reads curious. Anxious reads like someone pacing back and forth while typing.

Most texting mistakes stem from overthinking, too little pause, and the quiet urge to manage how the message will be received. This simply requires you to keep things light enough that the message can breathe. Let's consider a few scenarios:

The one-message advantage

Most good texts could stop after one sentence, or two at most. Anything beyond that usually starts turning into a performance.

Clean:

"Good meeting you earlier."

Still clean:

"Good meeting you earlier. Hope your week's going well."

Now we're sliding:

"Good meeting you earlier. Hope your week's going well. I don't usually do this, but I figured I'd reach out. Anyway, yeah, just wanted to say hi."

Nothing terrible happened, but the weight changed. The message went from presence to explanation.

A simple check before sending:

Would you say all of this out loud in one breath? If not, trim it.

When enthusiasm starts tripping over itself

Energy matters, interest is attractive, but overflow usually isn't.

Interest:

"Had fun at trivia. We should do it again sometime."

Overflow:

"Had SUCH a good time at trivia 😂 😂 😂 *honestly haven't laughed like that in forever bro, that was wild, next time we HAVE to do it again for sure!!!"*

Same message but very different feel.

When excitement spills into capitals, stacks of emojis, and exclamation points doing parkour, it starts reading less like confidence and more like nervous momentum.

One exclamation point is friendly.

Two is enthusiastic.

Five is a public service announcement.

The paragraph problem

If your message needs a scroll bar, pause. Paragraph texts usually come from:

- Nervousness
- Over-explaining
- Trying to steer the outcome before it happens

Screens are terrible places for speeches, so before sending, ask:

If this were a voice note, would I apologize halfway through? If yes, shorten it.

Shorthand, emojis, and stickers

Shorthand works when it matches how you actually talk. "lol," "yeah," "for sure," and "sounds good" feel natural because they are. However, over-stylizing usually backfires. Random abbreviations, forced slang, or trying to sound younger than you are tend to feel off quickly. Emojis can help with tone, but they should decorate the message, not carry it.

Clean:

"Sounds good 👍"

Now we're doing too much:

"Sounds good 😂 💧 🙌 😎"

Stickers are similar. One sticker after shared context can land, whereas multiple stickers in a row feel like you dropped your phone. If you wouldn't do it in real life, don't do it through text.

Follow-ups that stay human

One follow-up is normal; two starts to feel like pressure, but then three turns into a situation you didn't ask for.

Clean follow-up:

"Hey, all good if you're busy. Just checking in."

Not-so-clean:

"Hey man, just following up in case you didn't see my message. No worries if not. Totally understand if you're busy, just didn't want it to seem like I forgot."

That's anxiety trying to negotiate safety. If there's no response after a clean follow-up, let it rest.

Timing matters, but tone matters more

Daytime texts tend to feel lighter, whereas late-night essays tend to feel heavier, even when the intention is harmless. Memes work best when they connect to something already shared.

Good:

Sending a meme about a joke you already laughed about.

Confusing:

Sending a random meme with no context and hoping it lands. If you need to explain the meme, it wasn't the move.

When to stop typing

Stop if you're:

- Explaining why you sent the message
- Apologizing for texting
- Pre-empting every possible reaction
- Typing faster than you're thinking

Send less. Let space do some of the work.

What actually lands

Short.

Clear.

Optional.

"Thought of this and figured I'd send it."

"If you're around later, let me know."

"No rush at all."

These work because they don't corner the other person into a response. Remember, texting isn't where connection is built but where rhythm is tested. When rhythm exists, even simple messages move things forward. However, when it doesn't, nothing you add will manufacture it.

Keeping texts light protects your dignity and keeps you open to what's actually available, and that's the win.

Let It Land

At some point, your effort meets quiet. A message doesn't get answered when you expected it to. A plan fades without explanation. Something that felt present one week simply doesn't carry into the next. That moment matters, not because of what happened, but because of how you respond to it.

This is where many people start negotiating with silence. For instance:

- Re-reading messages.
- Replaying tone.
- Wondering what could've been adjusted.

That habit doesn't bring clarity, it pulls you away from yourself. The work here is simpler and harder at the same time. Accept what's in front of you without turning it into a story.

Things change, and that's okay. Not everything that opens is meant to continue, and not everything that pauses needs an explanation. A single follow-up can make sense when it's clean and unforced. After that, space usually speaks more clearly than persistence. You need to understand that there's a difference between showing interest and trying to rescue momentum that isn't there.

Running into someone again after silence doesn't require a reckoning. A simple greeting keeps things human. No reference to what didn't happen, and no tension carried forward. You don't need to close every loop for your life to keep moving.

Furthermore, missed connections are part of how alignment reveals itself. Each one clarifies what fits and what doesn't, without diminishing your willingness to reach out again. The men who build strong circles learned to adjust accordingly. They stay open, keep extending lightly, and trust that the right connections don't require force.

Letting things land the way they do is what ties this journey together. You learn to start conversations without pressure, extend without chasing, text without overreaching, and accept outcomes without hardening. That posture carries forward, and the rest follows naturally.

CHAPTER 5:
FINDING YOUR PEOPLE

"Community is much more than belonging to something; it is about doing something together that makes belonging matter." — Brian Solis

There's a shift that happens when you stop searching for connection in theory and start placing yourself where people already gather. Friendship doesn't begin with effort or personality but with context. The rooms you walk into shape the relationships that become possible.

- Most adult friendships form in ordinary places.
- Cafes where the same faces appear each week.
- Classes where people learn side by side.
- Groups that meet around a shared interest without needing a big reason to exist.

These environments carry qualities that matter. They allow people to cross paths naturally, return without friction, and grow familiar over time in ways that don't need to be engineered. All of this is essential, and we'll unpack it properly as we move forward.

Finding your people starts with noticing where life already has a rhythm. Spaces that welcome return visits. Activities that don't demand performance. Places where showing up again feels natural instead of awkward. When you place yourself in these environments, connection stops feeling like something you have to manufacture.

Choosing rooms with intention changes everything. Some spaces quietly support connection through their structure and the people they attract. When you learn to recognize those environments, meeting people stops feeling like effort and starts feeling like placement.

What follows is a closer look at the environments where connection tends to take root, and how to move through them in a way that feels natural and unforced.

Hidden Third Places

Friendship often grows because people keep crossing paths in the same places. Spaces that sit outside of home and work naturally invite this. Cafes, breweries, hobby spots, small gyms, game stores, dog parks, places like these quietly gather people who are comfortable staying a while. That willingness to linger is where things begin.

Third places work because urgency fades. Nobody arrives with a prepared speech, and no one needs the interaction to go anywhere specific. You show up, do your thing, notice the same faces again, and familiarity starts doing its quiet work.

Think about a local cafe where the barista recognizes regulars, and the same people drift in around the same hours. Showing up consistently is enough for your face to become part of the room. From there, conversation grows naturally, following recognition rather than trying to create it. The same thing happens in the places we mentioned. People come back because they enjoy the space, and relationships form almost accidentally because paths keep crossing. No pressure. No forced introductions. Just proximity doing what it does best.

A simple way to start is to map your week instead of your social life.

- Where do you already go when you're not trying to meet anyone?
- Where do you relax, train, study, or kill time?

Those places are often better starting points than somewhere you have to hype yourself up to attend.

Pay attention to rhythm. Certain spots move to their own patterns: the Tuesday evening crowd, the Saturday morning regulars, the people who always arrive a few minutes before closing. Showing up at the same time, again and again, carries more weight than trying to be everywhere at once.

Being a regular is about consistency and ease. A nod to the staff, a quick comment about the playlist, a smile exchanged with someone you've seen before. Over time, these moments accumulate naturally, without effort or intention.

There's also an unspoken skill here, knowing when to let the space do the talking. Not every visit needs a conversation. Some days you just show up, do your thing, and leave. Ironically, that restraint is often what makes future interactions feel natural.

If you're wondering where to start, look for places with built-in reasons to talk. Trivia nights. Open tables. Community boards. Hobby nights. Anything that gives people a shared reference point without demanding performance.

And yes, sometimes it's as simple as becoming the guy who's always there when the doors open or always there when they close. Familiarity is underrated.

Third places increase the likelihood of connection by reducing friction and making presence easier. You step into a room that already has its own momentum, where interactions tend to emerge naturally rather than needing to be sparked from scratch.

That's where friendship quietly starts.

DIGITAL-FIRST SPACES

Some spaces exist in the world around you, others exist quietly on a screen, but both work in similar ways.

After spending time in places where familiarity grows through repeated presence, the same pattern begins to show up online. Have you ever joined a group digitally, watched the conversations roll by for weeks, and felt connected before saying a single word?

Names start to feel familiar, and the jokes begin to make sense. You notice who shows up consistently and who fades after the first burst of excitement. Nothing obvious has happened yet, but something has already begun beneath the surface. That quiet familiarity is the part people tend to overlook. Digital spaces don't replace real connections, they prepare them. They let you observe before you enter, learn the group's rhythm, and understand the tone without needing to announce yourself. By the time you speak, you're already oriented.

Meetup groups, Discord servers, local forums, and even niche group chats all work similarly. They gather people around a shared interest, then give them time.

- Time to watch how conversations move.
- Time to see who's consistent.
- Time to notice which spaces feel welcoming and which feel forced.

Most men underestimate how much groundwork goes into before the first in-person meeting. It shows up quietly through reading threads, reacting lightly, and appearing in small, consistent ways. These moments rarely feel like progress in the moment, yet familiarity is already forming long before introductions ever happen.

When digital spaces work well, the transition offline feels almost anticlimactic. You walk into a room and recognize names, faces, or voices you've already encountered. The ice was cracked days or weeks earlier, quietly, without pressure. The key is approaching these spaces the same way you'd approach a good third place. You don't rush in or try to dominate the room, but you simply arrive, notice the flow, and let yourself settle into the environment. Consistency matters here, too, not intensity.

However, some groups won't fit, and that's fine. You'll sense it quickly. Others will feel easy to return to, even if you don't say much at first. Those are worth paying attention to.

Digital-first spaces reward patience more than performance. Familiarity grows through steady presence, through showing up often enough that names, voices, and rhythms begin to settle. When that happens, meeting in real life feels less like a jump and more like the next natural step, a continuation of something already in motion. From there, the question shifts from whether a connection is possible to where that connection has room to deepen.

After that orientation settles in, this is where things get practical.

Setting up a profile that actually works

Think of your profile as a quick snapshot, not a pitch. A few real interests you genuinely spend time on. One line that hints at how you like to spend your weekends or evenings. Enough texture for someone to recognize you, not enough to feel curated.

Examples that work:

- "Weekday gym, weekend coffee walks, trying to get better at cooking."

- "Remote worker, usually outside on weekends, into board games and long walks."

What tends to be missed:

- Bios that read like resumes
- Inside jokes no one understands yet
- Trying to sound busier or more interesting than real life actually is

If it wouldn't come up naturally in conversation, it doesn't need to live in your bio.

Choosing groups that fit instead of groups that look good

Smaller, recurring groups usually beat large, one-off events. Look for signs of rhythm rather than hype.

Green flags:

- Regular meet times
- The same names showing up repeatedly
- Conversation that continues between events

Yellow flags:

- Constant new faces, no familiar ones
- Lots of announcements, little interaction
- Events that feel more promotional than social

Leaving a group quietly is normal. Filtering isn't failure, it's alignment doing its job.

Reading the Room First

You don't need to make a big entrance. Most connections happen in small, low-stakes ways.

Examples:

- Reacting to a post that genuinely made you laugh
- Asking a short, relevant question
- Adding a brief comment that fits the ongoing thread

Avoid:

- Redirecting conversations to yourself
- Long introductions
- Dropping messages that don't connect to what's already happening

Over time, names stop feeling anonymous. That's the signal that an in-person meet will feel natural.

When Digital Turns Physical

Group settings work best here because the structure already exists. You're stepping into something that's already moving.

Simple transitions:

- "I'm thinking of joining the next one."
- "I'll probably be there this week."
- "Might check this out if I'm free."

No big announcements needed because showing up does the work.

However, some spaces will feel natural almost immediately, and others won't invite return. That contrast is useful. You've already learned how to handle silence and misalignment earlier, so there's no need to linger here. What matters is noticing where return feels easy. Digital spaces that work tend to mirror good physical ones. You come back without friction, recognition builds over time, and interaction feels human once you're inside it. From there, the path forward becomes clear, not through effort, but through placement.

BEYOND SPORTS

Structured activity carries a quiet advantage. When people gather around something with shape and continuity, attention settles on the activity itself, and connection forms alongside it.

For years, sports have been treated as the default setting for male bonding. In practice, connection grows anywhere shared focus and return are built into the space. Some environments lean physical: rec leagues, climbing groups, running crews. Others lean strategic or creative: board games, chess clubs, tabletop nights, maker spaces. The category matters less than the rhythm they create.

Structure does most of the work. Regular meeting times, familiar faces, and a clear reason to show up remove the pressure to manufacture conversation. You participate, learn the cadence, and let rapport develop in parallel.

Participation carries more weight here than performance. Beginner-friendly groups, social leagues, and open game nights tend to produce stronger connections than spaces driven purely by competition. Contribution and reliability signal more than intensity.

Small acts of involvement accelerate recognition. Helping with setup, staying a few minutes after, rotating responsibilities, or supporting the group in practical ways builds trust without announcement. Over time, these gestures compound quietly.

Furthermore, most of these groups develop their own patterns, such as standing teams and recurring hosts. These are shared references that only make sense if you've been there a few times. Those patterns turn attendance into belonging without needing to label it.

Invitations surface naturally in this context.

- A mention of the next session.
- A comment about another group nearby.
- An easy suggestion to continue the conversation afterward.

You're stepping into momentum that already exists rather than trying to create it.

Some activities feel natural to return to, whilst others don't. That contrast is useful; paying attention to where participation feels easy saves energy and clarifies where connection has room to grow.

Ultimately, beyond sports and beyond competition, these environments offer something steadier: shared activity, repeated presence, and enough structure. This lets connection develop at its own pace.

Shared Purpose

Some spaces make conversation easier by giving it somewhere to land. When people show up to do something together, the need for small talk fades. Attention shifts to the task, the class, the shared interest. Connection grows in the background.

This is where volunteering, learning environments, and niche groups quietly outperform almost everything else. They bring people together around purpose or identity, and both create familiarity faster than intention alone.

Volunteering and learning environments

Working alongside people changes the tone immediately. You're not there to impress anyone but to contribute, learn, or help. That shared focus creates a natural entry point into conversation without forcing it.

Volunteering works best when it aligns with something you already care about. Animal shelters, food banks, community gardens, neighborhood cleanups, and youth programs. Skill-based volunteering does the same thing in a different register. Helping a nonprofit with a website, coaching a local team, and teaching a workshop. Essentially, repeated interaction and shared responsibility do most of the relational work for you.

Classes and workshops offer a similar effect. Cooking classes, adult education courses, coding bootcamps, art workshops. Projects and assignments give people a reason to interact. You're solving something together, comparing notes, learning side by side. Conversation follows naturally.

Transitions don't need to be elaborate. Simple extensions are enough:

- "Are you coming to the next one as well?"
- "We usually help pack up after this. Want to join?"
- "There's a service project happening next week, I'm thinking of going."
- "We meet again on Thursday, I'll probably be there."

When there's a shared activity, these moments feel normal rather than forced.

Niche groups and finding your people

Specificity changes everything. When a group is built around a clear interest or life stage, much of the explaining disappears. You don't need to justify why you're there because everyone already shares the context.

Dad groups, book clubs, vinyl meetups, sci-fi reading circles, craft beer tastings, walking groups. Libraries, community centers, specialty shops, and online forums often become the meeting points. These spaces attract people who already care about the same thing, which lowers friction from the start.

Joining or forming these groups doesn't require grand plans.

- A regular walk.
- A monthly book swap.
- A standing game night.

Proposing something small and repeatable is usually enough. Over time, repetition turns familiarity into belonging. Stories from these spaces tend to unfold seamlessly.

Tale for instance, a new dad starts a Saturday stroller walk and ends up with a few close friends.

An introvert finds his rhythm in a weekly comic book club.

Someone invites a few people from a tasting event to share bottles once a month. Nothing fancy happens here, but people just keep showing up.

Ultimately, purpose and specificity work because they remove guesswork. You know why you're there. You know what you share. From that place, the connection has room to deepen without being rushed.

As life shifts, sometimes the environment needs to shift too. New cities, new seasons, new routines all change the social map. Knowing how to rebuild from scratch becomes its own skill.

BUILDING A CREW WHEN YOU MOVE

Moving resets more than your address. It resets your social map, your routines, and the quiet familiarity you didn't realize was doing so much work for you. The mistake most people make is treating that reset like a waiting period instead of an active phase.

However, before the boxes are unpacked, there's already work that pays off later.

Study the environment

Every place has its own rhythm, and assuming it runs like the last one is how people end up confused, frustrated, or accidentally rude. Culture shifts by city, by neighborhood, sometimes by street.

A little research goes a long way. Look up:

- How people socialize.
- What time the city wakes up.
- Where people tend to gather.
- Whether weekends are built around family, church, sport, nightlife, or nature.

Skip this step, and you might walk in expecting tacos and leave with something that sounds similar but definitely isn't.

Online spaces help here. Local subreddits, Facebook groups, city forums, and neighborhood pages give you a feel for how people talk and what they care about. You'll notice patterns quicker:

- What gets recommended often.
- Which areas people defend passionately.
- Where newcomers usually get pointed.

Arriving with a basic understanding of the place makes movement easier. You recognize the rhythms sooner, avoid unnecessary missteps, and settle in without friction.

The first weeks

Once you arrive, the focus shifts to becoming locatable. Being seen regularly in a few places matters more than trying to meet everyone at once.

Pick a few anchor points early, places you return to often enough for familiarity to form. A cafe, a gym, a class, a church, one recurring activity where your face starts to register. Over time, these become reference points, and people begin to recognize you as part of the landscape rather than someone passing through.

Digital spaces matter here more than ever. Meetup groups, local Discords, WhatsApp groups, and event pages shorten the distance between outsider and participant. Showing up online first lets you observe, then arrive in person with context instead of guessing.

Information & Presence

Here's a quick illustration: Ben and Bean both moved at the same time. Ben did his homework thoroughly. Blogs, TikTok lists, Reddit threads, Google Maps pins everywhere. He knew where people went, what was popular, and which spots were "must-visits." His calendar stayed empty. Preparation quietly replaced presence.

Bean took a different route. He picked one place, showed up on the same day each week, talked to the same few people, and left without trying to maximize anything. He didn't have any spreadsheets or a perfect plan, but then familiarity did the heavy lifting. A month later, Bean wasn't busy; he was included.

Information opens doors by pointing you in the right direction. It tells you where people gather and what tends to matter in a place. Presence keeps those doors open by doing the slower work, showing up consistently, being seen, and allowing familiarity to form over time. One without the other stays incomplete.

Early conversations don't need weight

Early conversations work best when they stay grounded in the moment. A simple, situational exchange carries you further than explaining your whole story:

- "Still figuring the city out, this place was recommended."
- "Just moved here recently, trying to find a rhythm."
- "This is my first time here. How long have you been coming?"

These statements do two things at once. They place you honestly, and they invite local knowledge without asking for validation.

Build outward, not all at once

Recreating an old social life all at once rarely works in a new place. The pace shifts and the context changes. Starting small creates traction: one or two connections, one recurring space, one group that feels easy to return to.

As comfort grows, your map expands on its own. A new place gets mentioned, and an invitation surfaces. One routine overlaps with another, and momentum builds without being chased.

Essentially, every move comes with a settling period. Even the right places feel unfamiliar at first, and that doesn't mean they're wrong. It simply means you're new, so treat the early phase as placement. Curiosity keeps things light, but showing up where return feels easy does the rest.

Rebuilding a crew after a move comes down to placement and rhythm. When you show up in the right spaces consistently, familiarity does what it has always done best.

KEY TAKEAWAYS

What you've just read isn't only for people who are moving cities; it applies anytime your social world feels thin, disrupted, or ready for expansion.

1. Choose environments before choosing people

Connection follows context. Cafes, clubs, classes, digital spaces, volunteer groups, churches, and niche communities all do quiet work before you ever speak. Put yourself where return is easy, and repetition is built in.

2. Let familiarity lead

Show up often enough for your face, name, and presence to register. Recognition creates comfort. Comfort creates conversation. Conversation creates connection.

3. Use digital spaces as orientation, not replacement

Online groups, forums, and chats help you read the room before you enter it. They shorten distance and remove guesswork, but a real connection still forms through shared time and physical presence.

4. Start small and expand outward

Start with a small base, one recurring space, one activity, and one or two connections. Momentum grows through overlap rather than overload.

5. Pay attention to ease

The right environments carry a sense of ease. Return feels natural, conversation stays light, and that quiet pull becomes information worth trusting.

6. Stay patient through the settling phase

Every season of change carries an adjustment period. Familiarity forms with time, and placement comes before belonging.

These ideas are meant to travel with you. They apply across seasons, locations, and stages of life. When you place yourself well and show up consistently, connection grows the way it always has, slowly, naturally, and through shared life.

CHAPTER 6:
FROM FAMILIAR TO REAL

"People will never forget how you made them feel."
— Maya Angelou

Familiarity opens the door, but depth decides what happens next.

By now, the rooms are no longer strange. Faces repeat, names stick, and conversations start easily enough. This is the moment where the connection either levels up or quietly stays where it is.

Relationships deepen because a few exchanges land with ease, a small truth is shared without weight, or time is spent side by side doing something ordinary together. The shift happens gradually, almost unnoticed, as trust accumulates through response rather than effort.

This part of the journey requires a different kind of attention. Not more confidence, not better lines, not even louder presence. What matters here is noticing pace, reading signals, and choosing when to lean in. Depth reveals itself through reciprocity, through curiosity reciprocated, and through the way someone remains engaged when the conversation delves a few inches beneath the surface.

However, some connections invite more, whereas others settle comfortably where they are. Either way, both outcomes carry information. Learning to recognize the difference keeps energy well placed and expectations clean.

We need to explore how conversations shift from polite to personal, how trust forms in small, unforced moments, why doing something together often matters more than talking it out, and how to tell when someone is ready to move from acquaintance to crew.

Most of this happens naturally when you slow down enough to notice what's in front of you.

When Small Talk Stops Working

Most conversations begin on familiar ground, work, schedules, the surface details that make an exchange easy to enter. That layer has a role. It helps two people orient to each other, find footing, and establish comfort before anything deeper is required. What matters is noticing when that layer has done its job.

You can feel the moment when repeating the same questions starts to flatten the exchange. The answers come quickly. The energy stays polite but contained. Nobody is bored, but nothing is moving either. That's usually the signal, not that something is wrong, but that the conversation is ready for a different kind of turn.

Depth tends to emerge in smaller ways, through questions that carry a bit more care and through the patience to stay with an answer just a moment longer.

As conversations settle, attention often shifts toward what someone cares about in the present. What's been occupying their thoughts lately, what they're anticipating, or something they've been quietly navigating. These topics tend to open space without weight, inviting a more human exchange that still feels easy to carry.

Shared context adds stability. A group you both belong to, an activity you keep showing up to, or a moment you've already experienced together creates continuity. Referring back to something familiar gives the conversation a spine, and that continuity allows more personal ground to open naturally.

Humor also matters because it lets people relax without having to explain themselves. A quick story about a first job that went sideways, a work-from-home moment that didn't go as planned, or a small everyday mishap often does more than a serious question ever could. It shows texture. Someone laughs, adds their own story, and suddenly the exchange feels shared rather than polite. That moment of ease usually comes before anyone would call it vulnerability.

However, what guides the moment is response. Someone picks up what you've offered and adds to it, asks a follow-up, or brings in a detail of their own. That's movement. Other times, the reply stays short, and the conversation settles back into neutral ground. That's information too. Paying attention to how the exchange breathes tells you more than trying to steer it.

Small talk serves as a bridge. Moving through it at the right pace allows conversation to shift organically, keeping the connection mutual and unforced as it deepens.

Those signals shape what comes next. When the rhythm stays open, the conversation has room to deepen. When it tightens, letting it rest keeps things intact and prepares the ground for the next layer.

DEPTH

Picture a group of guys standing around after an event, jackets half on, nobody in a rush to leave. The conversation is light, jokes flying, surface stuff. Then one of them laughs and says he almost didn't come out tonight because he'd had a rough week. He shrugs it off, changes the subject, and keeps smiling. Nobody stops the conversation, but something shifts.

That's how real depth usually shows up. It slips in sideways while everyone is relaxed enough to let their guard down. It could be a throwaway comment, a half-laugh followed by something honest, or a sentence that wasn't meant to carry weight, but does.

Think about how conversations actually unfold when you're comfortable with someone. You're talking about work, or the game, or something you both just experienced. Then someone mentions they almost didn't come out tonight. Or that they've been struggling to stay consistent with something they care about. The moment passes quickly, but it changes the room's temperature.

What makes these moments work is their size. They don't require reassurance or demand a response. They simply reveal a corner of the person that hadn't been visible yet. That kind of honesty feels safe because it doesn't overwhelm the space. Most men instinctively sense this, even if they've never named it. Big emotional speeches tend to shut rooms down, and small, well-timed truths tend to open them up. One invites pressure, whereas the other invites presence.

You can see it in the response. Someone nods and adds a detail of their own, or they smile differently, or the conversation slows just enough for something real to settle in. Sometimes nothing happens at all, and the topic moves on, and that's part of the signal too.

The skill here isn't sharing more but noticing what size fits the moment. When someone offers a little, meeting it with a little keeps the exchange balanced. When the room stays light, letting it remain light preserves trust. Depth grows through proportion, not intensity.

Over time, these moments stack, albeit not as dramatic revelations but as quiet confirmations. You start to recognize who can hold a bit of honesty without flinching and who prefers to keep things at the surface. Neither response is wrong, but both are informative.

This is how connection deepens in real life. It's not always through planned vulnerability or emotional dumps, but through ordinary conversations where something real is allowed to appear, then respected. The men who become crew are usually the ones who know how to recognize that moment and treat it gently when it arrives.

SHOULDER TO SHOULDER

There's a certain honesty that only shows up when nobody is facing each other directly. You see it in cars, garages, kitchens, gym floors, and half-finished projects, where hands stay busy and conversation moves in and out without pressure. Something about doing something together loosens the grip people usually keep on their words.

Think about a long drive. The road hums underneath the tires, music low enough to ignore, eyes forward. You're not watching each other, you're sharing direction. Somewhere between traffic lights, one of you says, "Work's been weird lately," not as an invitation for advice, just as a statement that wants air. The other nods, maybe says, "Yeah, same," and keeps driving. Five minutes later, the conversation drifts back and circles again, a little deeper this time, because the space already feels safe.

That's shoulder-to-shoulder connection. The task carries the weight, so the words don't have to. Silence feels natural because it belongs to the moment, not to discomfort. When someone speaks, it lands softly, without the feeling that it needs to be resolved or fixed.

You see the same thing when people work together to fix something. One guy tightens a bolt, the other holds the light. Someone laughs and says, "I swear, I used to be better at this," and the other replies, "We all think that," without missing a beat. A minute later, while still focused on the task, the first guy adds, "Honestly, I've been trying to get my life back into some kind of rhythm lately." Nobody stops working. Nobody makes a big deal out of it. The conversation keeps moving, but something real has been placed on the table and quietly accepted.

Walking side by side works the same way. On a trail, the terrain sets the pace, conversation breaking and resuming naturally. Breath gets heavy, jokes come out uneven, thoughts surface and disappear. Someone might say, "I didn't expect this hike to be this hard," and then, after a few steps, add, "Kind of how this year's been," followed by a half-smile. That's not a confession, it's a truth slipping out while the body stays occupied.

These moments don't need eye contact or dramatic pauses. They need time and shared movement. Cooking together, lifting weights, setting up chairs before an event, volunteering for something mildly inconvenient. The activity keeps the energy grounded, which lets honesty show up without stealing the spotlight.

What gives these settings their power is how optional everything feels. You can talk, you can stay quiet, you can joke, you can drift. Nobody feels trapped in the moment. That freedom makes people more willing to say what's actually on their mind, because there's no sense that it needs to turn into a conversation about feelings.

If you listen closely, you'll hear how this plays out in real dialogue.

"Man, I almost skipped tonight," someone says while packing up gear.

"Yeah?" the other replies, still focused on what he's doing.

"Just been off lately."

"Yeah, I get that," comes back, followed by a pause, then, "Same here, honestly."

That's it. The moment passes, but it leaves a mark. Over time, these small exchanges add up, then you start noticing who stays after the task is done, who keeps showing up, and who shares a little more each time without being pushed. Those patterns matter far more than any single deep conversation.

If you want to create more of this kind of connection, think less about what you're going to say and more about what you're going to do together. Choose things with built-in rhythm, a regular workout, a standing game night, a shared project, or a walk after work. Remember that you're not engineering vulnerability but building a container where trust can accumulate naturally.

This is where many real friendships take root, but side by side, moving in the same direction, letting life be talked about while it's still in motion. That's where connection feels earned, steady, and real.

THE WINGMAN EFFECT

This usually happens without a plan. You show up somewhere because one guy said, "Pull through, it'll be chill." You don't know who's coming. You don't know the room. You're already half deciding how long you'll stay.

Then you arrive, spot the one familiar face, and everything settles. He gives you a nod, maybe a quick dap, says something like, "You made it," and goes back to what he was doing, nothing dramatic, but your body relaxes. You're not auditioning, you're just there.

That moment matters because it connects directly to what came before. Shoulder-to-shoulder connection builds trust in motion, side by side, without pressure. The wingman effect is what happens when that trust starts to travel. Familiar ground makes unfamiliar rooms easier to move through.

Picture arriving at a casual get-together where you only know one person. He spots you, gives a nod, says, "Glad you made it," and keeps talking. Nothing flashy happens, but your shoulders loosen. You're already anchored. When he brings you into another conversation, he offers just enough context for things to move forward naturally.

"Hey, this is Mark. We train together. He's the guy who never skips leg day."

Mark laughs, adds his own comment, and the exchange immediately has texture. Nobody's starting from zero. The introduction gives the conversation a direction instead of a script.

Good wingmen understand this instinctively. They don't manage the interaction or play hype man. They offer a light frame, a shared interest, a small reference point that lets two people stand next to each other without an awkward setup.

"You two both hike early mornings," someone says while handing out coffee. "I figured you'd get along."

That's usually enough. The rest unfolds on its own.

What's happening underneath is a transfer of ease. When trust already exists between two people, some of it spills over into the space around them. The room feels less evaluative and more open. Nobody's trying to prove anything, and that's when curiosity has room to breathe.

This effect becomes even clearer in group settings. Having one familiar ally nearby gives you freedom to move, to step away, to rejoin without vanishing. You can drift through conversations knowing there's always a place to land. That sense of safety makes people more present and more willing to stay engaged.

You can hear it in the small moments.

"Stick around," your friend says quietly while refilling his drink. "I want you to meet someone."

A few minutes later, you're laughing with someone new about something unexpected, and the conversation keeps going even after your friend steps away. That's the handoff, subtle and unforced.

There's also an awareness that develops in healthy groups. People notice who's hovering at the edge, who hasn't been pulled into the circle yet, who looks interested but unsure where to enter. Small adjustments, shifting a stance, opening the circle, sliding a chair over, keep the space welcoming rather than closed.

"You want to jump in?" someone asks, moving aside.

That simple invitation changes the energy.

Bringing different parts of your life together often deepens connections on both sides. An old friend meets a newer one. A gym buddy joins a casual dinner. Shared moments create overlap, and overlap builds familiarity faster than isolated one-on-one interactions ever could. Over time, these overlaps form something sturdier than a collection of separate friendships.

- People recognize each other across settings.
- Conversations resume without warm-up.
- Trust builds through shared reference points rather than constant explanation.

It's worth paying attention to who naturally carries this energy. Some people make others feel included without trying to control the room. They create space rather than take it up. Those traits tend to remain consistent and often signal that someone fits well in a crew.

At the same time, not every connection needs to be pulled into a group. Chemistry still matters. When effort stays one-sided, plans keep falling through, or interest never quite returns, that information is useful. Letting those connections rest keeps energy available for the ones that grow with ease.

What begins to form through moments like these, is a different social shape.

1. Familiar faces stop feeling isolated.

2. Introductions carry context.

3. Rooms feel easier to enter because someone already knows where you stand.

When friendships begin to overlap without being forced, and people help each other move through rooms instead of guarding their corner, the connection starts to feel steady. That's how crews form, through shared ground that widens over time.

Group Chats

At some point, once people start overlapping and seeing each other in different settings, a group chat usually appears as a convenience. Someone says, "Let's just make a chat," and suddenly there's a shared thread connecting moments that already exist offline.

In this context, group chats matter because they sit between encounters and they carry momentum from one hangout to the next. They aren't the relationship itself, but they quietly influence whether the connection keeps moving or slowly stalls.

The chats that work tend to stay close to real life. They surface when plans are being made, when someone follows up, when a photo from last time gets dropped without commentary. The conversation comes and goes, but the thread stays relevant because it's attached to people who actually see each other.

Most issues show up when the chat starts floating without an anchor. Messages pile up with no direction. One or two people carry the energy. Plans circle but never land. When that happens, the problem usually isn't effort; it's that the chat no longer reflects anything happening outside of it.

A healthy group chat feels optional. You can dip in, step out, come back later, and nothing breaks. When someone suggests something concrete, coffee, a walk, or a game night, the chat briefly wakes up, does its job, then quiets down again.

That rhythm matters. The chat supports the friendship instead of competing with it. When it stays light, grounded, and tied to real moments, it keeps people connected between meetups. When it starts carrying weight it was never meant to hold, it fades on its own. Paying attention to that balance keeps the connection clean and lets the chapter move forward without dragging everything into the digital space.

SPOTTING THE SIGNALS

At some point, the room gets fuller.

You've met more people, shared a few moments, noticed that names come quicker and jokes land faster, and from the outside, it all looks like progress, yet underneath that movement, a quieter question starts to carry more weight than anything else.

Who is this actually worth building with?

Not everyone you vibe with is meant to come along for the long run, and that's not a failure. That's part of the sorting process. Connection expands first. Discernment follows.

Reciprocity

Most men don't say, "Hey, I'd like us to be friends." They show it sideways.

It looks like quick replies that don't feel rushed. Someone remembering a small detail you mentioned weeks ago and bringing it back up like it mattered. An invite that isn't overly planned but clearly intentional.

"Yo, a few of us are grabbing food after the gym, you down?"

You'll notice it in the effort that moves both ways. You suggest something once, and they suggest the next thing. You miss a hangout, they circle back later instead of letting it disappear. You walk away from conversations feeling steady rather than confused.

That ease is usually the giveaway. Crew energy doesn't feel dramatic. It feels mutual. On the flip side, there's a familiar pattern most guys recognize instantly. You're always the one initiating. Plans sound good in theory, but never quite land. Replies come late, if they come at all. Nobody's rude, but nothing deepens either.

That doesn't mean anyone's doing something wrong. It just means the signal is clear.

Trying to force chemistry where it doesn't exist drains energy fast. Letting those connections sit where they are keeps space open for the ones that naturally grow.

Choosing Depth Over Familiarity

Some people feel comfortable quickly. They're funny, they're around, and they fill the silence. That can be great, but familiarity alone doesn't always translate to depth. Depth shows up in smaller, quieter ways. Someone checks in after a rough week without needing details. Someone lingers after everyone else leaves. Someone says, "That actually makes sense," when you share something real instead of brushing past it. Sometimes the clearest sign is what happens when nothing is planned. You run into each other randomly without an agenda, and yet the conversation still holds.

Other times, the signal shows up through absence. You stop reaching out, and nothing fills the gap. That's information too, and it saves you from guessing.

There's also a kind of humor that belongs here. The inside joke that forms without trying. The shared glance across a room when something awkward happens. The ability to laugh at the same nonsense without explanation. That kind of alignment is hard to fake.

Choosing who to invest in comes down to attention. Energy tends to follow what's returned, and time naturally settles where it's welcomed.

By now, the patterns start to feel familiar. You know what mutual effort looks like. You know what drifting feels like. You've seen how trust builds in motion, how rooms open with the right presence, how momentum carries from one moment to the next. What's left for you now isn't effort, it's choice.

1. Choosing to lean into the connections that hold their shape without forcing.
2. Choosing to let others stay light without trying to turn them into something else.
3. Choosing to build with people who show up, not just once, but again.

That's how a crew takes form. Quietly, naturally, and over time.

CHAPTER 7:
CONNECTION & CONSISTENCY

"Most things don't fall apart. They fade." — Ernest Hemingway

A lot of friendships don't end with blowups or falling outs. They just taper off, and for many valid reasons too. Life fills up in ways nobody really plans for. Work stretches past the hours you promised yourself you'd log off. Days blur into routines that leave very little margin at the end. You think about replying to that message, even type a few words, then tell yourself you'll come back to it once things slow down, but unfortunately, they don't. What felt recent quietly becomes distant, not because the connection didn't matter, but because nothing demanded your attention loudly enough to protect it.

Most men know this drift well. You still respect each other. You'd still laugh if you ran into one another tomorrow. There just wasn't a clean moment where things stopped, so the distance feels strange, unfinished, like a conversation paused mid-sentence.

That middle space is where most friendships are quietly shaped. Not at the start, when everything feels easy, and not at the extremes, when something explodes, but in the ordinary stretch where nobody is trying very hard and nobody is doing anything wrong.

What carries connection through this stretch are small signals that say you're still in each other's orbit.

1. A quick check-in without an agenda.
2. A habit that doesn't demand perfect attendance.
3. The understanding that silence doesn't mean something broke.

Earlier, a connection was built through showing up. Here, it's shaped by how you return. Not with pressure or explanations, just with enough consistency to keep things familiar. This is where friendships stop feeling fragile and start feeling durable.

The Long Game

At some point, every friendship leaves the exciting phase. The one where plans happen fast, replies come instantly, and everyone swears they'll stay locked in forever. That phase is fun, but it was never meant to last.

Real life eventually shows up with a calendar in one hand and responsibilities in the other. Work ramps up. Someone moves. Someone becomes a parent. Someone's energy just isn't what it used to be. Suddenly, seeing each other every week turns into "we should link soon," and that sentence starts carrying more weight than anyone admits.

This is where most men get it wrong, not because they don't care, but because they quietly expect momentum to maintain itself. When it slows down, the assumption creeps in that something's off. Maybe the friendship wasn't that solid. Maybe people are drifting. Maybe it's better to leave it alone.

That assumption makes sense at first glance, but it doesn't really hold up once you look at how real friendships survive over time. Momentum was never meant to carry the whole weight. It's what gets things started, what makes the early days feel easy and automatic, but the long game is what decides whether anything actually stays.

Think about the friendships that have lasted in your life. Not the loud ones or the ones built purely on proximity, but the ones that survived distance, busy seasons, and long gaps without resentment creeping in. Chances are, they weren't held together by constant contact or regular updates, but by the fact that both people understood that absence didn't cancel connection.

You see this everywhere once you start paying attention. Two friends who only catch up every few months but fall straight back into rhythm. Old teammates who barely talk, yet show up without hesitation when it matters. Guys who don't need daily check-ins to know the bond is still solid.

That kind of durability doesn't happen by accident. It grows out of adjusted expectations and a shared understanding that connection can stretch without snapping.

The long game mindset accepts that friendship changes shape over time. Early on, consistency looks like frequency. Later, it looks more like reliability:

- Knowing that when someone does reach out, it's genuine.
- Knowing that silence isn't personal.
- Knowing that effort doesn't have to be loud to be real.

There's also a bit of humor in this phase, especially when you look back. Remember when staying up late talking felt effortless? Now you need a recovery day after one late night. Remember when plans were spontaneous? Now they require at least two calendar checks and a prayer that nobody's kid gets sick.

That shift is part of growing up. Life changes pace, responsibilities stack, and friendships have to stretch to fit the shape of reality. The real risk shows up when a slowdown gets misread as the end of something. When that assumption settles in, friendships quietly drift into memory, not because anyone chose distance, but because expectations never moved with the season.

Here's a simple reflection worth sitting with for a moment. Who in your life still feels familiar, even if you don't talk often? Who could you reach out to without needing to explain the gap? Those names usually point to connections that already understand the long game.

The goal here isn't to recreate early momentum or force things back to how they were. It's to let relationships mature without abandoning them, and to allow distance without disconnecting. Also, to keep the door open without standing in it.

Once that shift happens, everything else becomes lighter. Reaching out feels normal instead of awkward, gaps stop feeling like failures, and friendship starts to feel less fragile and more forgiving. That's the foundation everything else builds on.

Staying in the Loop

Once the long game clicks, the next question is simple and practical: how do you stay connected without turning friendship into another task on the to-do list?

Most of the time, keeping things going comes down to choosing moments that can survive real life, moments that don't collapse when someone's late, tired, broke, busy, or just not in the mood. This is the moment when timing and energy line up.

A monthly breakfast is a good example. Early enough that it doesn't hijack the day, casual enough that nobody feels underdressed, and infrequent enough that missing one doesn't feel like a failure. Someone floats it without ceremony, something like,

"I usually grab breakfast on the first Saturday anyway, if anyone wants to join, cool."

It lands casually, like an open door that doesn't ask for commitment.

Weekly runs work the same way. Same time, same rough plan, no attendance taken. The consistency does the heavy lifting, so nobody has to. Some weeks it's two people, some weeks it's five, some weeks it doesn't happen at all, and nobody spirals about it.

The way these ideas are introduced matters more than the ideas themselves. When it sounds light, it stays light. When it sounds flexible, people actually show up. Most of the time it's less, *"We should lock this in,"* and more, *"I'm doing this anyway if you want to jump in."*

That phrasing removes pressure before it even has a chance to creep in.

Rotating hosts helps for the same reason. One person doesn't end up carrying the whole thing, and nobody feels like they're imposing. One month it's someone's kitchen, the next month it's a cheap spot down the road, the next month it's coffee and a walk. Familiarity stays, effort stays spread out.

You'll also notice that the rituals that last leave room for imperfect participation. Someone misses two months in a row, then shows up as if nothing happened. Someone pops in late, leaves early, or just sends a message saying, *"Can't make it, catch you next time."* That kind of flexibility keeps the connection warm instead of brittle.

There's a subtle skill here that shows up over time. Staying in the loop looks less like constant contact and more like small reminders that people are still welcome, a quick check-in, a photo from last time, or a simple message saying, "You were missed," without loading it with guilt.

It often sounds simple. "We're grabbing food after the gym if you're around." "I'll be there around nine if anyone's keen." "Next month, same idea." These aren't scripts as much as habits of speech that keep things easy. Over time, this works because nobody has to prove interest or keep up appearances. The structure does enough of the work that people can come and go with ease. When life gets noisy, the door stays open, and when things calm down, stepping back in feels natural.

That's the quiet power of staying in the loop. It keeps the connection alive without squeezing it, and it gives friendships somewhere to land when everything else feels full.

Busy Seasons, Loose Grip

By now, you've already seen how connection survives when it's allowed to breathe. Earlier moments showed that momentum fades, rhythms change, and lasting relationships learn to move with that reality instead of fighting it. This is where that understanding gets tested.

- Life speeds up without warning.
- Schedules crowd out margin.
- Energy gets redirected toward whatever is loudest or most urgent.

The gap doesn't come from conflict or neglect, it comes from compression. What matters here isn't preventing the gap, it's how you read it. That difference has very little to do with effort and everything to do with posture.

A few things help here, and they're simpler than most people think:

- **Lower the contact bar, not the care.** During heavy seasons, staying connected often looks like less talking, not better talking. A quick message, a shared joke, or a reaction to something familiar keeps the line warm without asking for more than you have to give.

- **Combine connection with what you're already doing.** Catching up doesn't always need its own time slot. It can happen on a walk, during a workout, while running errands, or on the drive between commitments. Sometimes the best conversations happen when nobody has to clear their schedule for them.

- **Name the season lightly.** A simple, "Things are a bit wild right now, but I'll circle back," does more than disappearing quietly. It removes guesswork without turning the moment into a big conversation.

Awkwardness usually grows when nothing is said, and everyone starts filling in the blanks. A missed invite turns into a story, and a delayed reply turns into doubt. Most of that tension dissolves the moment someone acknowledges reality out loud, even briefly. It doesn't need to be heavy, it often sounds more like:

- "Hey man, this month's been chaotic, but I've been meaning to reach out."

- "I'm in a bit of a tunnel right now, I'll resurface soon."
- "Life's been crazy lately, just wanted to say I haven't forgotten you."

Those kinds of messages don't demand anything in return; they simply keep the door open.

There's also a maturity that shows up when people stop keeping score. You'll have seasons where you carry the connection a bit more, and seasons where the other person does. Over time, it evens out if the foundation is real.

The loose grip matters because pressure kills goodwill faster than distance ever will. When friendship starts feeling like another obligation to manage, people pull back without always knowing why.

Keeping things warm through busy seasons comes down to staying human when life gets full, trusting that connection can bend without breaking, and knowing when to hold on lightly instead of tightening your grip.

Conflict, Repair, and Knowing When to Let Go

Tension shows up in friendships the same way it shows up everywhere else. A joke lands the wrong way, a message goes unanswered, or someone feels brushed off and doesn't say anything. Nobody announces there's a problem, but the energy shifts. Most guys recognize this moment immediately. You feel it before you think it. Something's slightly off, and now you're deciding whether to ignore it, joke past it, or name it. Ignoring it works sometimes, but other times, it lets small things harden into distance.

However, when something does need to be addressed, it doesn't necessarily require a big sit-down or emotional unpacking. It usually works best when it's handled early, plainly, and without an audience. It often sounds like:

- "Hey, quick thing, something felt a bit off the other night. Wanted to check in."
- "I might be reading this wrong, but I wanted to clear it up."
- "Can we rewind that moment for a second?"

The tone usually does more work than the exact wording. Keeping it calm and straightforward lowers the temperature and makes it easier for the other person to stay open instead of defensive.

Owning your part goes a long way here. Not in a heavy way, just enough to lower the temperature.

- "My bad, I dropped the ball on that."
- "I should've handled that better."
- "Didn't mean for it to come across that way."

Most conflicts between men don't need a winner. They just need a sense of closure so things don't linger and quietly reshape the relationship.

Once things are named, the goal is movement, not resolution. You're not trying to agree on everything or replay the whole situation. You're just getting back to neutral, so the friendship doesn't stay stuck.

Sometimes the moment passes easily. A quick laugh, a nod, and it's done. Other times, the tension keeps resurfacing. That's usually a sign to pause.

Not every dynamic needs fixing. Sometimes space does the job better. Stepping back doesn't require cutting someone off or burning a bridge; it can be as simple as fewer plans, lighter contact, or allowing the connection to settle where it naturally wants to sit.

You usually feel the difference before you can explain it. Conversations lose their ease, or effort starts leaning in one direction. You walk away feeling more drained than steady. Those signals matter; they're information worth paying attention to. Letting a friendship loosen doesn't erase what it was. It just acknowledges what it is now.

When distance makes sense, keeping things respectful matters. It often sounds simple and honest.

- "I've appreciated our time. Life's just pulled us in different directions."
- "No hard feelings at all. Just a different season."

Sometimes, after time passes, a connection circles back. When that happens, the question worth asking isn't whether it feels familiar, but whether it feels healthy.

Reconnecting works best when it's grounded in the present, not driven by nostalgia. Shared values now matter more than shared memories then. And sometimes, the right move is to do nothing at all, letting things fade without forcing a conclusion.

Handling conflict well, and letting go well, both come from the same place: Maturity. This is the ability to care without gripping, to speak without escalating, and to walk away without resentment. That's how friendships stay clean, even when they change.

No Loose Ends

Picture a group of men standing around a parking lot after something that mattered. The plans are technically over. Cars are unlocked, engines are about to turn, and nobody's rushing off just yet. A few jokes get traded, and someone mentions a small tension from earlier in the night, not sharply, just enough to clear the air. It's acknowledged, brushed off, and the moment settles. Everyone leaves lighter than they arrived. That's what healthy endings look like.

Not every connection needs to be intensified, repaired, or carried forward at full strength. Some benefit from a quick adjustment. Others from a bit of distance. A few from being allowed to end without turning into something heavier than they ever were.

What matters is how those moments are handled. Address what needs addressing while it's still small. Step back when things feel strained, rather than forcing closeness. Let certain bonds rest without rewriting the past or questioning whether they mattered.

A simple check is often enough:

- Does this connection feel steady or tense?

- Does effort move both ways or tilt consistently in one direction?
- Do interactions leave energy behind or take it with them?

Those answers tend to surface on their own when things are kept honest.

Friendships that age well aren't perfect, and they're not permanent by default. They stay healthy because friction is addressed early, space is respected when needed, and endings are allowed to remain clean. Nothing gets dragged out longer than it should, and nothing meaningful is dismissed out of fear.

That posture keeps relationships grounded. It frees attention, preserves respect, and makes room for the connections that still fit.

That's how a man moves forward without carrying unnecessary weight.

CHAPTER 8:
SUPPORTING MEN

"The strongest man in the room is often the one carrying the most quietly." — unknown

From a young age, men learn how to occupy space in a very specific way.

1. Be reliable.
2. Be composed.
3. Be the one who shows up and handles things without needing much in return.

Strength becomes something practical, something measured by how little disruption you cause while carrying weight. Over time, that expectation settles into the body. Emotions get sorted internally before they ever reach the surface. Stress becomes something you work through alone, and confusion gets turned into action. Even joy is often kept contained, expressed through shared activity rather than words. None of this feels like suppression in the moment. It feels like maturity. It feels like doing what's required.

Many men grow up surrounded by people, yet still experience long stretches of isolation that don't look like loneliness from the outside. They're present at work, present at home, present in responsibility, but rarely invited into spaces where presence includes being unguarded. The inner world keeps moving, but it stays largely unshared.

This is where misunderstanding often begins. From the outside, things appear fine. From the inside, there's a constant hum of pressure, expectation, and self-management. Men adapt by becoming efficient with their emotional energy. They ration it and direct it toward solving problems, providing stability, and staying useful.

That adaptation shapes how men relate, not just to others, but to themselves. Connection often forms around doing rather than discussing. Trust grows through consistency and shared experience. Support shows up sideways, through presence, humor, and action, rather than long conversations about what's being carried.

When that kind of connection is missing, the weight doesn't disappear; it redistributes. Partners, families, and homes feel it. One person slowly becomes the primary container for everything that never found another place to land.

Understanding this landscape matters. Not so that anyone can fix it, manage it, or take responsibility for it, but so the quiet mechanics of male connection can finally be seen clearly. When those mechanics are understood, support becomes lighter, relationships breathe easier, and men are no longer expected to carry everything alone without ever naming the cost.

What follows, in that space, is a closer look at how men bond, how support actually helps, and how the people around them can create room without taking control.

Why Male Friendship Matters

There's a visible difference between men who have a place to put weight and men who don't. It shows up in posture, patience, and how much room they give the people around them. One carries himself with a quieter steadiness. The other moves through life slightly compressed, always holding something back.

Research has tried to measure this for years. Men with strong peer bonds tend to live longer, recover faster from stress, and show lower rates of depression and isolation-related illness. Their nervous systems regulate differently. Pressure dissipates instead of accumulating. Responsibility feels shared, even when life is heavy.

What rarely gets named is how this plays out at home. When a man's entire emotional world funnels into one relationship, the weight intensifies. Partners feel it as constant proximity, unspoken expectation, or emotional saturation. Not because either person is doing something wrong, but because the system itself has no overflow.

When male friendships are present, something subtle shifts. Conversations at home become lighter. Frustration finds release elsewhere before it hardens. Laughter returns without needing a reason. Men show up less guarded because they've already been seen in other spaces.

Male bonding often looks ordinary from the outside: time spent fixing something together, long stretches of shared activity that don't need explanation, humor traded in shorthand, and trust built quietly through repetition rather than disclosure. The value lies in returning to the same space again and again, not in intensity or emotional display.

These spaces give men room to be unfinished without needing to explain themselves. Presence doesn't require performance, and over time, that permission settles into confidence.

This is why the absence of male friendship carries consequences that reach far beyond loneliness. Without other places for pressure to go, stress concentrates, irritation surfaces faster, and emotional weight quietly shifts onto partners, children, or work. The strain spreads through the system, even when no one stops to name it.

When men have access to real peer connection, the effect radiates outward into the spaces around them. Homes feel steadier, relationships gain breathing room, and children observe a model of shared strength rather than silent endurance. Male friendship doesn't remove responsibility, it redistributes it, and that redistribution leaves everyone involved standing on firmer ground.

Encouragement Without Control

Support can either lighten a man's load or quietly make it heavier. The difference often has less to do with intention and more to do with posture.

When encouragement respects autonomy, it creates room. When it slips into management, even with good intentions, it starts to feel like supervision. Most men sense that shift immediately, not as criticism, but as pressure.

Healthy encouragement usually comes across quietly. It sounds like trust rather than instruction. There's room to choose, room to move at his own pace, and an unspoken sense that he's capable of finding his way into connection without being steered.

You can usually hear the difference in how it sounds.

- "There's a trivia night at that spot you like. Could be fun if you want to check it out with someone."
- "I know you've been meaning to catch up with those guys. I can cover things here if you want to go."
- "You seemed lighter after hanging out last time."

None of those moments comes with an expectation attached. There's no need to explain what happened, no pressure to prove anything worked. The invitation is offered, and then it's left alone.

Things usually start to feel off when support slowly gives way to coordination. Suggestions keep coming. Check-ins start sounding like reminders. A pause gets read as avoidance.

Without anyone intending it, encouragement begins to feel like something that has to be managed rather than accepted.

A simple internal check can help keep things clean:

- Does this offer preserve choice?
- Does it assume capability rather than hesitation?
- Does it leave room for a no without consequence?

When the answer stays yes, support tends to land well.

Validation shows up most clearly when effort doesn't immediately lead anywhere. Reaching out, showing up once, trying something unfamiliar, even when it feels awkward, all of that counts on its own. Those moments matter regardless of how they land.

Hearing something as simple as, "That took guts," or "I'm glad you tried," often does more than celebrating a full social calendar ever could.

Making space is part of encouragement as well, and it usually shows up in practical ways. Time gets protected. Calendars shift a little. Responsibilities are covered without resentment, and time spent with other men isn't taken personally.

That kind of support tends to steady a man rather than pull him away. He comes back more present because the space was given freely.

When encouragement stays light and respectful, grounded in trust, it supports connection without trying to replace it. The posture stays simple, space is made, and nothing needs to be forced.

Raising Boys Who Value Crew

Pause for a second and picture a boy growing up, not in theory, but an actual boy you know, a son, a nephew, a kid in your family or community. Pay attention to what he absorbs long before he understands what anyone tells him. He watches who adults make time for, whether friendships quietly disappear once life gets busy or stay woven into the week in small, ordinary ways, and whether connection is treated like a luxury or something that simply belongs in everyday life.

Boys learn friendship by watching it lived, not by being instructed on it. When a father steps out for time with his friends and comes back lighter, calmer, and more present, that lesson lands without a word being spoken. When a mother protects space for her own friendships, the message is clear. What gets communicated in those moments is simple and lasting.

- Relationships are allowed to take up space.
- Responsibility doesn't require isolation.
- Growing up doesn't mean growing alone.

Think about how often boys are left to figure this out on their own. They're expected to be independent early, resilient quickly, and emotionally composed without ever seeing what a healthy connection actually looks like in motion.

Connection doesn't need to be formal to be formative. It shows up in car rides where conversation drifts naturally. In shared projects that take time and cooperation. In backyard games, team sports, music sessions, or building something together. The activity carries the interaction, and meaning slips in quietly while hands are busy.

Conflict shows up too because it's an inevitable part of life, and this is where the lesson deepens. When boys see adults address tension calmly, without humiliation or avoidance, they learn that disagreement doesn't threaten their sense of belonging. When apologies are offered immediately and accepted without scorekeeping, repair becomes normal instead of scary.

How things are handled carries more weight than what gets said. Casual check-ins, small acknowledgments, and moments where something feels off can be named and settled without turning into a scene, all of which shape how boys learn to relate. That's emotional literacy forming quietly, without speeches or sit-down talks.

There's also an unspoken layer that boys pick up about vulnerability. They learn what strength looks like by watching how adults carry emotion in real time. Feeling doesn't weaken them; it gives shape to their inner world. Learning how to carry emotion without being overwhelmed builds stability, and connection becomes something that anchors character rather than eroding it.

Ask yourself a few honest questions:

- What version of friendship is being modeled day to day?
- Where does connection feel normal, and where does it feel squeezed out?
- How often do boys see adults repair, not just endure?

What all of this builds toward is a sense of belonging. Not boys who perform openness, but boys who grow up knowing they have a place to land.

When community is modeled early, men don't have to relearn it later. They grow into it already knowing that strength and connection were never opposites in the first place.

There's one more layer that deserves care, because it shows up early and tends to linger.

Many boys grow up absorbing messages that were never meant to harm them, but often do. Words like "man up," "toughen up," or "boys don't cry" usually come from a place of protection or frustration, not cruelty. Still, they leave an impression. Over time, emotion is treated as something to outgrow rather than something to learn to carry.

What lands isn't just the phrase itself, but the tone behind it. Discomfort around emotion teaches boys to hide rather than understand what they're feeling. Seeking support starts to feel like a failure instead of something normal. The instinct becomes to handle things alone, even when connection would help.

A quieter, steadier message changes how boys learn to relate to themselves. Struggle can be acknowledged without being dramatized, tears don't need commentary, and asking for help doesn't require justification. When emotion is allowed to exist without embarrassment or punishment, vulnerability starts to feel like a normal part of being human rather than a liability.

Friendship fits naturally into that picture. Needing other people doesn't weaken resilience, it reinforces it. Belonging gives boys room to practice honesty, conflict, repair, and trust long before life begins to demand those skills under real pressure.

Make Room

What sits underneath all of this is not a technique or a role, but an environment. Men tend to do better when connection is allowed to exist without commentary, pressure, or management. Partners feel lighter when support doesn't turn into supervision. Families stabilize when emotional weight has more than one place to land. Communities strengthen when men aren't expected to carry everything in isolation.

Making room happens across all of those layers. It shows up when encouragement sounds like trust. When time with friends isn't treated as a threat to commitment. When space is offered without strings attached. When effort is noticed, even if outcomes stay modest.

It also shows up in what gets modeled. Boys watching adults prioritize connection, learn that responsibility and community can coexist. Men seeing other men supported without being controlled learn that asking for space doesn't cost them dignity. Women watching that balance take shape no longer feel the quiet pressure to be everything.

Nothing here requires forcing closeness or fixing people. The work is lighter than that. It's about keeping pathways open, letting connection move where it wants to, and allowing support to remain shared rather than concentrated.

When that environment exists, men settle, relationships breathe, and communities hold more without strain. That's what helps connection last, not effort alone, but room.

CONCLUSION

At some point, real life takes over again. The book gets closed, the day keeps moving, and the same mix of work, responsibility, energy, and distraction comes back into view. That's where all of this is meant to live.

Connection improves when you notice yourself inside it. Notice where you are stretched thin; where you're withdrawn without meaning to be. And where you still have room to show up, even if it looks different than it used to.

- When your life shifts, your relationships shift with it.
- A new job changes your rhythm.
- A heavier season narrows your margin.
- Fatigue shortens your patience.

None of that means you're failing at connection; it means the conditions have changed, and the way you move has to change with them.

In moments like that, the instinct is often to either push harder or pull away completely, but neither usually helps. What helps is adjusting your aim.

- Smaller moves
- Fewer expectations
- Staying in motion without trying to recreate an old version of closeness.

If reaching out feels awkward, it usually means you haven't done it in a while, not that it's the wrong move. You don't need the perfect message or the right timing. You need something simple enough to send without overthinking, something that keeps the line open instead of trying to explain everything at once.

When effort isn't matched, resist the urge to turn that into a story about yourself. Some connections are lighter by nature, and some only work in certain seasons. Learning where to invest is part of building a steady circle, not a personal shortcoming.

As life fills up, connection doesn't vanish, it compresses. It becomes less frequent, less elaborate, and more dependent on routines that can survive inconsistency.

Now that is adaptation: you're not looking for constant access, you're looking for continuity.

Ultimately, use what you've read as a reference when something feels off. Retrospect to the parts that match your current season and let the rest sit. This isn't something to execute all at once, it's something you return to when your footing changes.

Nothing here requires you to become louder, more outgoing, or more impressive. The work is just as simple as:

- Paying attention.
- Choosing timing over force.
- Knowing when to lean in and when to let something breathe.

That's how this fits into real life: as a way to move with more awareness when connection starts to matter again.

The Field Kit

Eventually, there comes a point where thinking about connection stops helping, and movement matters more. That's where this part comes in.

Not as a system to follow or steps to complete, but as a way to get your bearings when something feels slightly off. When you're not sure where to place your energy. When a relationship needs less force and more feel. These are the kinds of adjustments you make in real time, not all at once, and not the same way every time.

1. The Positioning Check

Before reaching outward, check where you are standing. Connection always reflects context. Workload, energy, season, stress, and margin all shape how much you can realistically give. When those conditions shift, relationships respond accordingly.

A few grounding questions:

- Where is most of my energy going right now?
- Which connections feel easy to step into, even briefly?

- Where does effort feel natural instead of forced?
- What am I trying to revive that no longer fits this season?

Clarity keeps resentment from building.

2. The Reach

Reaching out doesn't need buildup. Most of the time, the moment gets heavier because too much meaning is attached to it. The simplest move usually works best. Think of it as tapping someone on the shoulder rather than sitting them down for a conversation. You're letting them know you're there, not asking them to account for the distance.

Messages that land well tend to sound like how you'd actually speak:

- "You crossed my mind earlier. Hope you're good."
- "I've got some space this week if you feel like catching up."
- "This reminded me of you. Are you still into that?"

Nothing needs to be tied up before you send it. Don't treat it like you're attempting to revisit old ground or filling in the space between then and now. You're simply trying to open a lane and see if there's movement.

However, the most important thing here is 'tone'. Your tone does most of the work here. Messages that sound like you tend to land better than ones that sound rehearsed. When it feels easy to send, it usually feels easy to receive.

3. The Invitation

Time together holds better when it has shape. Movement, shared tasks, and a clear container make conversation easier without forcing depth.

This can look like:

- walking together
- training or working out
- cooking or eating
- fixing something
- sitting somewhere familiar with no agenda

The activity carries the interaction. Connection has room to show up without being placed under a spotlight.

4. The Rhythm

Relationships stay alive through recognizable patterns rather than constant contact. A rhythm gives people somewhere to return without pressure.

Useful rhythms tend to be loose and repeatable:

- a familiar coffee spot every few weeks
- a standing game night that people drop into when they can
- a short check-in text that doesn't require a long reply

Remember, consistency matters more than frequency. Returning feels easier when the path is already there. So just focus on cultivating the rhythm, the rest is determined by that.

5. The Depth Gauge

Not every connection wants the same level of closeness. Some bonds stay light and functional, whereas others slowly deepen. The challenge usually starts when closeness gets pushed faster than the relationship can comfortably hold. You can read this in the movement of a conversation if you stay attentive. Ask yourself:

- Does curiosity get returned, or do questions keep landing on one side of the table?
- When something slightly personal comes up, does the room stay relaxed, or does the energy tighten and drift?
- Over time, does sharing feel mutual, or does it somewhat turn into one person carrying most of the weight?

You notice these things in real time. Someone circles back to something you mentioned weeks ago. A pause lands easily instead of feeling strained. A moment of honesty sits in the room without derailing the conversation. Those small details tell you how much weight the connection can carry.

Matching pace keeps connections intact. When depth grows at a pace both people can sustain, it doesn't need guarding or explanation; it just settles in and holds on its own.

6. The Repair Window

Friction shows up in every long-standing relationship. What matters is how quickly it gets addressed.

Small conversations, handled early and without heat, prevent tension from hardening.

This can sound like:

- "Something from earlier stuck with me. Can we clear it?"
- "I might be off here, but I wanted to check."
- "That landed strangely for me, probably not what you meant."

The aim is understanding, not winning. Closing the loop keeps the relationship steady.

7. The Release

Not every connection needs to be carried forward with the same weight. Over time, you can feel when something has started to pull more than it gives back, when contact leaves you drained, or when effort keeps leaning in one direction.

When you notice that shift, you don't have to announce it or turn it into a moment. Most of the time, you adjust quietly.

- You reach out a little less.
- You keep plans lighter.
- You stop reviving conversations out of obligation and let them breathe on their own.

Over time, the connection settles into the level it can actually hold without creating tension.

Handled this way, distance doesn't have to turn into resentment. Space can exist without hostility, and by not forcing what no longer fits, you leave room for the connections that still feel steady to keep their shape. Essentially, you need to be okay with certain connections fading. It's an inevitable part of life, and trying to restore everything to how it was only leads to depression and unrealistic expectations.

8. When Support Helps

Support lands best when it feels like quiet confidence rather than supervision. The kind that assumes competence, leaves room to choose, and doesn't hover over the outcome. Most men sense that difference immediately.

In everyday life, this looks ordinary.

- Time gets protected without a running commentary attached to it.
- Space is made without keeping score.
- An effort is acknowledged for what it is, even when it doesn't turn into a big win.
- Someone sends the invite, someone shows up once, another tries something that feels a little unfamiliar, and then decides what to do next.

What steadies men in moments like these is trust. Trust that they can move at their own pace, adjust when things feel off, and figure out what fits without being steered or corrected. When encouragement carries that tone, it feels safe to accept instead of something that needs to be worked around.

Support at its strongest doesn't rush or crowd the process; it creates enough room for initiative to grow on its own. Over time, that room lowers the pressure, makes attempts feel lighter, and allows connection to develop without being forced.

9. Working With Professionals

When you're sitting across from someone who feels disconnected, the work usually starts long before strategy. Most men aren't confused about their situation; they already feel the gap. What they're carrying is hesitation, self-doubt, and a quiet fear of getting it wrong again.

The most useful conversations don't push for insight or emotional breakthroughs. They stay close to what feels possible right now. They help someone find their footing without putting them on display.

Questions that tend to open space sound grounded and ordinary:

- "Who feels easiest to reach out to these days?"
- "Where do you already feel somewhat comfortable showing up?"
- "What kind of interaction would fit the energy you actually have this week?"

The purpose is to help someone orient themselves without pressure. Progress often shows up in small, unglamorous ways. One message sent, one room entered, one attempt made without over-analysis, staying for a few minutes instead of pushing through discomfort until it becomes overwhelming.

When something feels awkward or doesn't land, it doesn't need to be turned into a lesson immediately. Sometimes it's enough to acknowledge that it happened and that the person stayed with it. That recognition builds trust in the process and reduces the urge to withdraw.

Over time, these small repetitions create familiarity. Familiarity lowers friction, and when friction eases, connection starts to feel less like a risk and more like something a person can step into without bracing.

10. Designing Supportive Environments

Connection grows more easily when the environment does some of the work. In workplaces, neighborhoods, and community spaces, this often comes down to creating situations where people can be alongside one another without needing to perform or explain themselves. Shared activity matters more than forced conversation. Familiar routines matter more than big events.

This might look like interest-based groups that people can join without commitment, recurring gatherings where showing up late or leaving early doesn't draw attention, or spaces that naturally break into smaller clusters rather than pushing everyone into the same interaction.

Designing environments this way lowers the cost of participation. When friction is reduced up front, people don't have to spend energy bracing themselves just to belong.

11. Threads

What gets modeled tends to get repeated. When boys see adults maintain friendships alongside responsibility, community becomes normal rather than optional. When connection is treated with respect rather than teased or dismissed, belonging settles in early.

Small exposures add up. For instance, invitations, shared projects, and letting boys witness repair, not just endurance.

In a nutshell, there are moments when circumstances change in your life, and that's inevitable. However, in times like that, it helps to have something solid to come back to.

Some of what follows will feel immediately familiar. Other parts will sit quietly until a later season pulls them back into focus. That's how this work tends to move, in layers, not all at once.

Connection holds when it's handled with patience and timing, when attention is placed carefully instead of spread thin. What fits becomes clearer when you stay honest about your current season, and the rest has a way of surfacing when it's needed.

AUTHOR'S NOTE

I'm writing this from a quiet kitchen table in a small town outside Pittsburgh, early on a Saturday morning, coffee going cold beside me, two kids asleep upstairs who'll be awake in about ten minutes and asking about breakfast. That's the life this book was written inside, not from some distant perch, but from the same kind of ordinary weeks most of you are living.

If there's one thing life has made clear, it's that people, seasons, and roles change. Sometimes people grow with you. Sometimes they grow away from you. Both can hurt in different ways. Losing people hurts, but so does standing in uncertainty, not knowing where you stand or how much to keep giving.

I've learned that every season comes with new personnel. Some stay longer than others. Some teach you something and move on. Fighting that reality only stretches you thin. Accepting it brings clarity. It helps you invest where effort is met, where presence is felt, and where connection has room to breathe.

This isn't just written for you. It's written for me too. There are more people out there carrying the same weight you are, holding things together quietly, doing what needs to be done, and rarely being asked how they're really doing. Sometimes all it takes is one reach, one check-in, one moment of honesty for things to shift.

Being a man was never meant to be easy. There's responsibility to carry, people to protect, and pressure that doesn't always get named. We hold families together, show up when it counts, and keep moving even when we're tired. But we were never meant to do that alone. Just like you hold things down for others, there are people meant to hold it down for you, too.

If you've made it this far, you're doing better than you think. You're paying attention. You're trying. That matters.

From my heart to yours.

REFERENCES

Angelou, M. (n.d.). *People will never forget how you made them feel.* Medium. https://medium.com/@treadmilltreats/people-will-never-forget-how-you-made-them-feel-d95d6bd9e6ee

Aurelius, M. (n.d.). *Be tolerant with others and strict with yourself.* Medium; Pragmatic Wisdom. Retrieved December 27, 2025, from https://medium.com/a-little-stoic-wisdom/be-tolerant-with-others-and-strict-with-yourself-marcus-aurelius-c4c1cec5fc94

Bruce Lee. (n.d.). *Patience is not passive, it is concentrated strength.* Substack; The Pen and Sword Journal. Retrieved December 27, 2025, from https://martialx.substack.com/p/patience-is-not-passive-it-is-concentrated?utm_campaign=post&utm_medium=web

Cleveland Clinic. (2023, April 11). *Amygdala.* Cleveland Clinic. https://my.clevelandclinic.org/health/body/24894-amygdala

Mother Teresa. (n.d.). *The most terrible poverty is loneliness, and the feeling of being unloved.* Goodreads. https://www.goodreads.com/quotes/50997-the-most-terrible-poverty-is-loneliness-and-the-feeling-of

Pavese, C. (n.d.). *We do not remember days, we remember moments.* BrainyQuote; BrainyQuote. https://www.brainyquote.com/quotes/cesare_pavese_109425

Salzman, D. (2025). amygdala | Definition, Function, Location, & Facts. In *Encyclopædia Britannica.* https://www.britannica.com/science/amygdala

Schumacher, H. (2019, March 17). *Why more men than women die by suicide.* BBC; BBC Future. https://www.bbc.com/future/article/20190313-why-more-men-kill-themselves-than-women

Solis, B. (n.d.). *Community is much more than belonging to something; it is about doing something together that makes belonging matter.* Medium. Retrieved December 27, 2025, from https://medium.com/@ifeomaudusk/the-importance-of-community-in-building-a-tech-career-path-b7cc2cab30e7

The Wingman Effect. (2025, October 21). NRB. https://nrb.org/event/the-wingman-effect-how-to-access-divine-wisdom-for-your-career-business-and-beyond/